What Can I Do About ~~Him?~~

Healing From the Trauma of My Husband's Pornography and Sexual Addiction

Rhyll Anne Croshaw

About the cover: *Gently up the Stream,* by Linda Curley Christensen.

If life is compared to a river, it is easy to imagine floating with the current gently down the stream. But if we simply go with the flow, disaster awaits. Every worthy goal takes constant, if gentle, effort to move upstream, and each individual must take responsibility for rowing their boat if success is to be obtained. – Linda Curley Christensen

So it is with sexual addiction and marriage; each person must take responsibility for their own recovery. Recognize that individual effort and commitment is required, both for the addict and the afflicted spouse. While each can support the personal recovery of the other, ultimately each person is responsible for their own success. Only then is there hope that the relationship can recover and the marriage can move *gently up the stream.*

Author's website: www.rhyllrecovery.com

Alstroemeria Blossom photograph provided by wholeblossoms.com.

Copyright © 2012 by Forward Press Publishing, LLC
All rights reserved.

Forward Press Publishing, LLC
P.O. Box 592681 • San Antonio, TX 78259
www.forwardpress.org

ISBN-13: 978-0-9819576-1-6

First Printing 2012
Second Printing 2013
Third Printing 2016
Printed in the United States of America

Contents

Part One: I Thought It Was About Him

My Story. 3
You Are Not Alone. 21
Choices. 33

Part Two: Working On Me

No Way But Through. 47
Boundaries: The Most Loving Thing I Can Do. 57
Forgiveness Is Not the Same as Trust 83
I Can't BUT He Can, and I Will Let Him 93
Gratitude in the Present Moment. 107
Self–Care and His Care 115
I'll Row My Own Boat 131
And They Lived Happily…One Day at a Time. 141

Appendix

Making the Decision 149
What About the Kids?. 169
Tara's Story 175
Recovery Road Maps. 181
Resources I Can Recommend 195

Acknowledgments

First and foremost I would like to thank my courageous, warrior-hearted husband. He has been totally open—willing to air his dirty laundry to the whole world—in an effort to shed light on the problem of pornography and sexual addiction. As I have read sections of this book to him, he has not even flinched at some of the most intimate and potentially shaming material. I am thankful to him for sharing his life and his struggles with me. I am grateful to be married now to a *real* man, a man in recovery.

Starting this book was a big hurdle and without the loving encouragement of Sara Israelsen Hartley and Craig Israelsen I may still be staring at a blank computer screen. They sat me down with a tape recorder and told me to talk; the rest is history. Likewise, I'm grateful for Ann Tolley and Kathy Whitaker, who for years have worked tirelessly beside me on the SA Lifeline Foundation and encouraged and supported this project.

Because I don't see myself as a gifted writer, I needed help. Angels were sent to turn what I thought was going to be a pamphlet into a book. Kristen Carr and KayLee Dunn have stuck by my side throughout the entire process. They have spent countless hours in my home office interviewing, transcribing, writing, organizing, editing, and praying alongside me. I am also grateful for the editing talents of Katie Pitts and Kristina S. and the encouragement and experience of Jenny Tolley. I also express gratitude to Bryan Crockett who gave of his expertise and inspiration to add professional touches and to make this message all that it should be.

I am eternally grateful for my children and their spouses, Paul and Diana, Amy and Jason, Megan and Sam, Spencer and Melanie, Tara and Luke, Preston, and Tanner, and for my parents Darwin and Barbara, who have been my personal cheerleaders throughout my life and throughout this process.

Finally, and most humbly, I thank the hundreds of women who share their heartaches, their miracles, and their journeys with me as we stand shoulder to shoulder as courageous and faith-filled women—warriors ourselves, in recovery.

Introduction

I struggled for over 30 long years to recover from the effects of my husband's sexual addiction, and I continue to work one day at a time. Writing a book has never been on my bucket list. Even when multiple individuals encouraged me to write about my experiences, I resisted. I don't see myself as a writer. However, as so many women are suffering from the devastating effects of pornography and sexual addiction, I want to offer my experience and my feelings of hope for recovery and joy to be found in our lives.

The purpose of writing this book is to help all people, men and women, recognize the need for an afflicted wife's healing; to give hope and tools for that recovery and healing; to share my own experience and hope for the recovery of the marriage and the family; and to share my belief that God's love for each of us is real, and as we come closer to Him we will find peace and joy.

As you read about my experience and the experiences of other women who are struggling with this affliction, you may find yourself triggered. You may feel pain, anger, and trauma as you compare the similarities and differences between these stories and your own. These feelings are more than justified due to the plague of sexual addiction in your life. I encourage you to continue to read and put into practice the healing behaviors outlined in this book. *When you change, your life will change.* That is the golden principle. The light that you gain and send out will attract more light and dispel darkness. That means that your spouse will either be drawn to you through his own recovery or choose a different path. Either way, you can be happy.

As I have worked on my own recovery, I have found an unexpected opportunity to develop my self-confidence, courage, and permission to be myself. I have learned to be authentic. This process has also brought me the gift of peace, knowing that I am loved, validated and directed by a Power that not only controls the entire universe but is involved in my life as well. You too can receive these priceless gifts.

In the first part of this book I tell my own story. As you read this, if it looks like I wasn't handling this situation correctly, I wasn't! But in order to understand where I am coming from you need to know my story. I next invite you to dispel shame in your life and come out of isolation. There are thousands of women who also feel bitter pain as spouses of sexual addicts and thus understand your agony in this affliction. Finally, I present the possible choices you are probably facing at this time. It is important to understand that we do have choices, but we need to make wise choices and understand the consequences of those choices.

In the second part, I provide specific principles that were necessary for my own recovery. These are the eight principles I began to use when I realized that I needed to stop focusing on fixing *him* and start working on *my* own life. Though frightening, the first principle is that *pain is the pathway to progress*. This is where we truly learn to dispel fear and live by faith. Next, *boundaries are for safety and for creating intimacy; they are not for punishment*. Third, *forgiveness is not the same as trust*. Early on in my marriage, I believed that forgiveness and trust were synonymous; however, by understanding the difference, I have come to find peace and serenity in my life. Fourth, *learn to surrender the things I cannot change to a Power greater than me*. Though I have always felt a connection with God, here was my opportunity to connect more deeply. Fifth, *practice gratitude in all aspects of your life,* in each day and each moment. This has been essential to my recovery. Sixth, as we feel God's love, we will learn to *care for ourselves as He cares for us*. The seventh principle is *my happiness is my own responsibility, and I cannot choose happiness or peace for anyone else.* Finally, I have found that *there is great joy in connecting with and being vulnerable with those I love and who love me.*

I have found that reading a book, though helpful, does me no good unless I put the principles into action. So, at the end of each chapter is a "journal page" to write your own feelings, thoughts, and commitments of things that you feel impressed to do.

My overall goal in writing this book is to share with you my path—though not perfect—to the healing, peace, serenity, and even joy I have found amidst the turmoil. Through these 8 principles I have found peace. I encourage you to read, integrate these principles, and "live one day at a time, enjoy one moment at a time."

Rhyll Anne Croshaw

www.rhyllrecovery.com

PART ONE

I Thought It Was About Him

MY STORY

With a name like *Rhyll* it is hard to be anonymous, so I choose not to be. I am at my best in kitchen-counter conversations with friends and family. I tell it like it is. My life is very messy at times; downright ugly at other times. But it is wonderful and beautiful most of the time.

Rhyll is a Welsh name meaning "a sunny place." Of course in my youth I wished to have a normal name like *Becky* or the elegant *Elizabeth*, but I came to terms with *Rhyll*. Now, I honestly like to identify myself with the meaning of my name. In spite of the adversities I face because of my husband's addiction I have become a sunny place for myself and others, working to shine in stark contrast with the choking darkness of sexual addiction. I want to shed some light on the path of recovery and healing for all women who experience betrayal and trauma due to pornography abuse and sexual addiction. This is my story, and I offer you hope through my experience.

Meeting Steven

I am the oldest of nine children, raised by loving parents who show their faith in Jesus by the guileless way they live. We were raised in extremely humble circumstances in the mountains of Montana, but we all felt loved

What Can I Do About ~~Him?~~ Me?

and connected as a family. We spent our summer days exploring the woods and building little playhouses. Sunday evenings were spent singing around the piano as a family. Our siblings were our best friends. The lack of material things didn't bother me most of the time. I loved to read, and we never had a television. It wasn't until I became an adult that I realized how sheltered I had been.

I met my husband, Steven, at church during my sophomore year at Montana State University, the university close to my home. I was studying music on a scholarship and teaching piano as a side job. I loved life and enjoyed my friends and experiences in college. I was not interested in marrying soon. I knew I could be happy no matter what life brought to me. I felt I could live life as a single woman, bless children by teaching music, and find joy and fulfillment.

When we met, Steven was working in Bozeman, Montana, and was scheduled to be there for only three more months before he would be transferred. He knew he didn't have much time to pursue a relationship, so when he decided that he was falling for me, he began to be serious pretty fast. After a few dates, he started talking marriage. By then, he was convinced that I was the one for him. Steven was charming, handsome, financially successful, played guitar, and sang beautifully. What was not to love? Still I was hesitant, and determined to ask God what I should do. I was serious and consistent as I prayed for divine direction. Just as consistently, I received answers of peace about continuing the relationship.

Three weeks after our meeting each other and becoming acquainted with both families, we became engaged. And soon after we got engaged, Steven left for his next work assignment—2,000 miles away. Our engagement lasted three months. During that time Steven came back for just one week; the rest of our contact was through phone and letters. In order to be wise in our decision we met with a marriage therapist to ask his opinion about our upcoming marriage and life together. His feeling was that we didn't know each other well and we were very young.

At hearing this I felt anxious, but I still trusted my answers. I realized that I did not know Steven really well from the short time we had dated, but I was determined to follow the inspiration that I felt I had received. I hadn't found anybody else who was marriage material for me. Steven was kind and admired by many people. He shared the same faith that I had grown up with and loved. We made a good match with our similar talents and interests. I recognized that I did want to marry him, and I did love him. We connected during that short time. He wrote me wonderful, loving letters, was very interested in me, and showed me love. Beyond my own hopes and Steven's loving actions, I truly felt that God approved of my decision to marry Steven, and in that I felt peace.

The First 13 Years

Steven and I were married March 22, 1973, in the LDS Temple in Logan, Utah, and immediately moved far away from my family. We didn't take time for a honeymoon; Steven was focused on getting back to work. Three days into the marriage, I discovered that he was often gone emotionally. I felt disconnected from him—like he was behind a brick wall. In spite of those feelings, we shared the company of good friends and played music together frequently. In our early years we purchased a small piano and refinished it together. Sometimes I felt connected, but many times I felt so alone.

In both our good and bad times, I missed the focus and attention Steven had paid me in our short dating experience. I went through several experiences in the first year of our marriage when I needed emotional support, but he did not make himself available. As a result of a traumatic experience, my first pregnancy ended in a miscarriage at four months. I sat on the floor at home with tears streaming down my face. Fears rushed through my mind: *What if I can't ever have children?* As my heart was shattering into tiny pieces, Steven turned on the TV.

At other times of trial, he buried himself in his work, whereas I wanted him to sit by me, hold me, and understand my pain. I didn't feel empathy from him at all. Steven often traveled for his work in sales, which meant I was frequently alone. Yet I was determined to be a loving wife, so I kept a spotless home and made healthy meals daily. Striving to "bloom where I was planted," I made efforts to take care of my own happiness by making good friends, teaching piano lessons, and making my home a comfortable place.

We eventually moved closer to our parents and soon thereafter had our first baby. I naturally started to focus on being a mother. Our next four children followed—all within five years. I was very busy and spent most nights awake with crying babies. But I found fulfillment. Once you have a baby or two, it's easy to put your focus on the children in order to deal with difficulties in the marriage. For me, it was a combination of distraction and responsibility. I really wanted to be a good mom. Though I continued to feel disconnected from my husband—which bothered me a great deal—I worked all the harder to care for Steven, our children, and our home.

We lived on a farm in Cache Valley, Utah, several miles from the next neighbor. In the summer, Steven would be home more often to mow the hay and sell it, but most of the year he would take off for two weeks at a time on business trips. When he returned home, we were happy to be together, and we worked together well on the farm. But at the same time, when I needed to talk to him he would tell me he was too tired. He made himself unavailable to me so often. One night I went out, laid myself down on the lawn, looked at the heavens and sobbed. I wondered that if I took the car and ran it off a cliff, would Steven even care?

Life at home was basically good, but I felt an undercurrent of unrest a lot of the time. Yet I still believed I could change my feelings of emptiness by just working harder. I read books on communication and marriage, hoping to find a solution. I even read the book that said if you got naked, wrapped yourself in plastic wrap, and met your husband at the door, that would do the trick. Actually, I thought it was ridiculous and refused to go that far, but I read the book thinking that if only I could get his attention somehow, it would fix our problems. I left little notes in his suitcase, made special dinners, and tried to have everything clean so that he would love to come home.

At my insistence, we saw a number of marriage counselors. The subject of sexual addiction never came up. Steven would tell each therapist that he felt our relationship was good and that he didn't have any dissatisfaction. He would say, "*I'm* not having any problems; I'm sorry *she* is." I left each session with more determination to work harder at my marriage. I felt that I wasn't enough for him. He was never an angry, mean, or critical person, so I never felt justified in being mad at him. I thought the problems were all about me; *he's fine, or at least he says he's fine.* But something *was* wrong and every effort to improve left me feeling more and more responsible, confused, and crazy. Thirteen years came and went.

The 1st Disclosure

In the middle of a sunny day in 1986, I was driving towards town when I passed Steven on the highway, headed home to find me. He flagged me down and said he needed to talk to me, so I got in his car. We drove out to the lake, parked next to it, and he proceeded to change both our lives.

Steven confessed to me that he couldn't live with himself anymore without a significant change; he had been living a double life. I was aware of one life, but the other was filled with loathsome betrayal. He told me he had been looking at pornography, frequenting strip clubs, and hiring prostitutes— for years. He said through tears that he was *so* sorry.

I sat in disbelief and total shock. I stared straight ahead and cried quietly. I felt such pain that I didn't want to let it out. Simultaneously, my heart was bursting and my chest imploded. My hands tingled. Around me the landscape looked sunny, beautiful, and peaceful. Inside me was utter destruction and chaos. I could see a few people in the distance, and I wondered how they could go on with life while I was dying.

I sat in silence while my husband disclosed that he had been involved with adult establishments and pornography—even before we were married; the prostitution came after. He never did any of it, he said, when he was in our home town. Only when he traveled was he this different person and escape back into the behaviors.

After over three hours of listening to Steven talk, I asked, "What are we going to do?" With remorse and determination he told me that he would talk with our church leaders and clear things up that way. Then he took me back to my car. That was that.

What Can I Do About ~~Him?~~ *Me?*

I drove home, wiped my tears, and fixed soup for dinner. I didn't know how to feel so I felt everything and nothing. I went through the motions of caring for my family because I didn't know what else to do. My trauma was so crushing that I couldn't piece my world back together. I didn't understand, couldn't understand. *How could I not have known? How could this person I adored so much be doing such revolting things?* It just didn't fit with who I thought he was. I simply could not imagine him—that man, that face—out there with a prostitute! I could not visualize the father of my children hungrily consuming pornography or experiencing some rush of being in a strip club. I couldn't match the person I thought I knew with this startling revelation. *This can't be the same person I go to church with, the father I'm so proud of, or the husband who has built this beautiful home for us!* The world I had been living in before this day was uncomfortable at times—but safe; then suddenly, my world no longer felt safe.

Steven did as he promised and immediately made an appointment with our church leaders. They expressed concern and love for both of us. He was given church discipline and counseled to work on repentance; I was counseled to work on forgiving him. Because we were such "good" people striving to do the right things, they told us that as we moved forward the Lord would help us and bless us.

For the first year, Steven made a real effort to be more kind to me and attentive. He was trying and working hard. There came, however, a gradual slide back to a state of disconnect. Again he buried himself in his work and started to travel—this time internationally. Though he was gone for about the same amount of time, he was much farther away.

I retreated to the world that I had grown up with: hard work and little money. He would call frequently, but I felt marginalized because I was home with all these little kids while he was off seeing the world. He was eating steak, and we were eating tuna fish. I often worried if I even had enough money to buy groceries, and wondered where he was really spending our money. During this time, we had our sixth and seventh children—a set of twins. Our lives were very busy and the days plodded on. When comparing my life to other women who had more visible and serious difficulties, I felt that perhaps my expectations were too high for a healthy and happy marriage. And so my life went on almost as if nothing had happened.

At the time, of course, I had no understanding of my own need for healing. I tried to bury my pain and fear because I believed that forgiveness was supposed to automatically include a restoration of trust. When I dared to ask Steven if he was okay, he would say he was fine and tell me that I needed to put it all behind me and forgive him. Other times, he would become irritated at this. He'd ask what my problem was, and why I couldn't just trust him. I felt he was being critical by not allowing me to have feelings.

I still felt disconnected but I believed his line that it was *my* problem and that *I* needed to be more kind and forgiving. *His* problem was apparently all gone. Whenever I brought it up, I thought that meant that I hadn't yet forgiven him. So I tried even harder to be an adoring wife. I felt that if I were just prettier, sexier, smarter, and more loving he would not be tempted to return to his offensive behaviors.

Six more years passed. In July 1993, Steven came home and announced that he thought we should move. He had been commuting to a consulting job for several months and felt it would be better for our family to relocate for a short time while he built a solid foundation with the company. I thought that it was a drastic thing to uproot our children and walk away from the home and farm we had worked on for 20 years, but I finally agreed. I did not realize at the time that Steven was actually trying to run from his addiction. He later told me that he thought that if he had us closer to him, daily, that he could escape the trap of his behaviors—enough for him to quit.

Within one week of "his announcement" we rented out our home in Cache Valley and moved two hours away from the safe and comfortable community we'd grown accustomed to. Our new house was on a cul-de-sac in the middle of Orem, Utah. It was absolutely claustrophobic to us. We lived within a few feet of our next-door neighbors, their children, and their children's toys. One neighbor child would even open the front door and ask if he could eat dinner with us! Coming from an 80 acre farm with natural boundaries, I felt that I had no control in this confined environment. The city was a culture shock for our entire family, and we all suffered in that place.

What Can I Do About ~~Him?~~ *Me?*

Three months after our arrival in Orem, I marched into the office of each of my kids' schools, pulled them out, and re-enrolled them in schools in Springville (a smaller town to the south); then I found a different rental there. We moved four times that year, which kept me busy. We never moved back to our farm in Cache Valley. The moves were painful for all of us. As for Steven, I would learn later that these moves were not enough to resolve his festering problems.

The 2nd Disclosure

Ten years after his first disclosure to me, Steven came forward again. It happened one beautiful fall morning in our bedroom as he was getting ready for work. I had been out fixing breakfast and getting the kids ready for school, and had just walked back in our bedroom to make the bed. Steven came out of the bathroom and tearfully told me he'd been at it again, beginning with those dreaded words, "I need to talk to you."

For nearly three years following his first disclosure, he had been able to *white knuckle* his way through, telling himself over and over that he shouldn't act out, trying to use sheer willpower to stop his addiction. But as he continued to travel, he started viewing pornography again, eventually went to strip clubs, which escalated to hiring prostitutes. By the time he came forward again, he'd been acting out for seven years. After he told me, I was so angry that I wanted to yell at him but I didn't want my children to know something was wrong. So instead, I raised my voice in a piercing whisper and demanded, "Why can't you stop doing this? You are throwing away your entire life for a 'mess of pottage'!?" He told me through his tears that it was not my fault, and that he wanted to change. In my frustration and outrage I kept repeating, "why?" But he couldn't answer.

In my keep-it-together mode, I checked on the kids and got them off to school. Then I dragged myself into the bathroom, locked the door, and sobbed with my face on the cold floor. When I finally came out, Steven was waiting in the living room—tearful and remorseful. That day I cycled through pulling myself together, doing what I needed to do, and retreating to the bathroom to cry. Overcome with grief, I spent hours sobbing and pleading for God to hear me and show me what to do.

I felt shocked and alone, but this time I was also angry. At times, I wanted to beat the literal hell out of him. After all, I was true Montana stock; I had the grit required to rise to nearly any challenge. I was used to muscling through on my own because I thought that was the only way. I took care of our seven kids and the farm, alone, while he was gone. I had twins at age 37. I laid the sod on our lawn, planted the bushes in our yard, laid tile in the bathroom, and textured and painted the walls in our home. I packed my family up and moved into four different houses in a year. My desire for stability came out in hard work. I figured that if I didn't do it, who would? I considered myself to be a strong woman who could take care of things. So when Steven came forward this time, my reaction was different.

At the first disclosure, I had focused on trying to forget and had been fairly passive. This time was much more confusing as I tried to assert myself more. Sometimes I loved him and wanted to take care of him, but I still hated what he was doing—the infidelity, the lies, the deceit, and the double life. When he would come home in the evenings, I would see him and instantly feel upset. Even though his presence brought out a toxic reaction in me, I desperately wanted to be loved and validated by him. We spent hours talking, yet never came to any conclusions. He felt shame, and I felt total frustration.

I wanted to shield our children from the pain in our marriage, but I knew that it was spilling over into the family. You cannot hide such pain from perceptive children. I cooked meals, cleaned, and carpooled to school, then sobbed on the way home. I forced myself to clean my house, and then would just lie down and cry because I hurt so much. Intense grief weighed on me every second. And my children sensed it.

It was because of our children that finances became a tipping point. That's where I felt particularly justified in being angry. I had been scraping every dime together, and he had been spending money on prostitutes. Though I've never been a violent person, the idea of beating him up with a baseball bat really became appealing. I could accept whatever he was going to do to me, but taking from my children was another thing. I felt

What Can I Do About ~~Him?~~ Me?

that he wasn't sacrificing for our kids, but I was. I was there every day trying to pull together a meal, but where was he? While traveling he would place a dutiful phone call to me at night, then do whatever he wanted the rest of the time. The financial safety of being provided for went away.

The year was 1997, the 150th anniversary of the Mormon pioneers' arrival in Utah. I read histories of the brave women who pulled small handcarts across the plains. One woman's story in particular touched my heart. Amidst snow and low food rations, she took her sick husband, put him in her handcart, and with her children alongside began pulling him across the miles of rocky terrain that lay ahead. I related to that story powerfully. I was likewise determined to put my sick husband in my handcart. I even explained in a family meeting that with God's help, we would make it through our challenges and difficulties. I knew it wouldn't be by just my physical strength, but I still believed I could fix it on my own. At times I thought, *"Steven, get your legs in. I'm doing all the work and you're lying back there with your legs hanging out. You're slowing this process down!"* I assumed I could pull everyone through with enough faith and determination on my part. In the end, this only left me frustrated.

As part of my effort to manage Steven's recovery, I started looking for help. A few years before, I had read a book titled *Willpower Is Not Enough* by A. Dean Byrd and Mark Chamberlain, on the *in*effectiveness of using willpower alone to enact change.[1] It seemed to shed some light on the possibility that my husband did not have control of his actions.

Dying for information, I began calling directory assistance to find the main author. When I finally found Dr. Byrd's number, I called him and told him our story. He explained that he had an 18-month waiting list, making it impossible to see him sooner. I was desperate though. He eventually offered one of his lunch hours the following week to meet with Steven and me. After listening to us, Dr. Byrd explained that my husband had an *addiction*; Steven was not capable of loving me—or anyone. We needed to treat his problems as an addiction. Finally, here was something that felt like truth.

---

[1] A. Dean Byrd and Mark D. Chamberlain, *Willpower Is Not Enough: Why We Don't Succeed at Change* (Salt Lake City: Deseret Book, 1995).

With this small glimmer of hope, I began to learn about addiction and my husband's history with it. Steven had been first exposed to pornography at the age of six. Knowing it was wrong, he gave his mother the magazine, but she didn't really respond. Even though he did not understand as a young child, he never forgot the feelings he had while looking at the pictures. He later searched for more such images, and then discovered the rush of masturbation.

His addiction had escalated during his high school years and into his young adult years. After he met me and was considering marriage, he went to his LDS bishop for help. Steven told him he had stopped his behavior, and the bishop counseled him to move ahead, put it all behind him, and not burden me [his fiancée] with the details.

After our lunch-hour session with Dr. Byrd, he referred us to another therapist closer to our home, but this new therapist did not specialize in sexual addiction therapy. "Don't think about it," the therapist told him. Steven was willing to go to therapy, but he didn't really take the initiative. I left each weekly session feeling we weren't making any progress, but I continued to hope for a miracle.

My husband then began attending a 12-Step support group. In my attempt to fix his problem, I went with him to the first two meetings—which I found out was a big no-no. I sat there and thought, *"I hope he's getting this!"* After the second meeting, someone took us aside and said, "Your wife doesn't belong here." Unaware that those meetings are closed to anyone who's not a sex addict, I was offended. I really wanted to help him fix his problem!

Steven, though, was actually glad that I was offended. Without me there to push him or hold his hand, he didn't have to go back. He wouldn't accept that he was an addict, or the label of one. Steven's denial, and minimization of his addictive behavior, were huge obstacles to any genuine recovery. Naively, I kept pulling him along to therapy and asking if he was okay.

Deep down, I still felt that nothing had ever gotten resolved. At this time, there was nothing available on sexual addiction that I knew of—no books, no resources, nothing. We told parents and some of my immediate family about Steven's behaviors. They and our church leaders were loving and kind, and again the church provided appropriate discipline, but no one knew how to *really* help us.

The 3rd Disclosure: Rock Bottom

After nearly a year, Steven announced that he was "fine" and that we no longer needed therapy. Life again went on as normal. The following years were very busy years for our family with teenagers, weddings, and grandchildren all flowing through our home. Steven's "white knuckling" approach kicked in again, and he fought hard to maintain his freedom from addiction. He stopped traveling, which he knew to be a trigger for "acting out" behaviors, and searched for a new job that would provide sufficiently for our large family and be fulfilling for him. Financially, things looked tough for us. But Steven finally found something that seemed a good match for his many talents, and life was good—mostly.

Eight more years passed, when on a beautiful Sunday morning in the fall of 2005, Steven sat down next to me in church and quietly told me he would not be able to participate in the service. I instantly knew what that meant. I thought, *Don't touch me!* I wanted to crawl under the church pew. The timing couldn't have been worse: I was about to play a musical number during the service, and then conduct a women's meeting later on. *I will just have to hold it together*, I thought.

I prayed for strength to get through my responsibilities that day, and to then have the courage to do what God wanted me to do. My eyes welled up with tears, but I didn't want to cry in church because I had too much to do. I thought, *I cannot believe this is happening again!* My immediate prayers were answered, and somehow I got through my obligations while maintaining a fairly stoic demeanor.

Later that day, Steven told me everything as we stood together on the front lawn of our home: he had been arrested for solicitation of a prostitute two weeks prior in a city 50 miles from our home. Even though he had gone to an attorney and paid $1,500 to get himself out of legal trouble, he could no longer live with his shame and guilt. For the past five years, he said, he had been acting out again, but the arrest was his rock bottom. He realized that he could possibly lose everything. He was very afraid that I would divorce him, that the children would reject him, and that he would lose his job. This shame and fear had kept him in hiding until now.

In that moment, I surrendered to God. I turned my hands and my tear-filled eyes up to heaven and said, "Take him. I can't do this anymore. I have done all that I know how to do. I can't do this!" It was my rock bottom as well. I felt as if someone had kicked the air out of me, but I didn't care. I wanted to retreat to my room and crawl under the bed where no one could find me.

"I know you must think that our marriage is over," he said, "and I don't blame you." After 32 years of this, I did think it was over, that I would no longer have a home, and that I would need to find a way to provide for my younger children. Steven determined to move his things to our camper in the backyard to sleep, and I was just fine with that. I really didn't want to be around him. We needed a separation at that point. In spite of the trauma, a strange sense of calm eventually settled over me.

One reason for the calm I felt was that I had actually been spiritually prepared for this moment. Prior to this disclosure, our daughter had returned from serving a mission for our church and was married a short time later. The world had felt lovely, and I was living a full life. I was really happy. So when Steven came forward this time, I could recognize that this was clearly *"his* stuff". Because it was *his*, I knew then that I couldn't change him or fix his problems.

My 15-year-old twin boys were the only ones home that day. Of course, they knew something was going on when I came into the house. Steven followed me in and told them, "I have been immoral, and I need to make some major changes." I held their faces in my hands and said, "I don't know what's going to happen, but I know God's going to take care of the three of us; it's you and me."

I no longer had the strength or motivation to pull my husband in my handcart. I also realized, finally, that my rescuing attempts had not made any difference in his behavior. In fact, perhaps I had unknowingly enabled and prolonged his addiction. I acknowledged that my husband was going to have to get out and walk on his own. That handcart had been unbearably heavy. This time, I was ready to completely surrender my control of the outcome.

There was only one place to go for help. As I pled with God to give me the answers, He kept saying, "Just hang in there. Just for today. Take care of your family. Keep praying." It didn't make sense at the time, but that was exactly what I needed to do. I had no clue what was going to happen; my life had become unmanageable. But I moved forward one small step at a time, and felt that a Higher Power was directing my journey.

Surrendering is still a daily process for me now, but from that moment on, my will was not in the way of anything. I had to give up my desire to fix and manage things. A strong marriage has always been a righteous desire of mine, and I believed that in time God would give those blessings to me. But I had to surrender the outcome of my marriage. Once I surrendered, it wasn't my job to fix it.

Though this was Steven's third disclosure to me, this was only the beginning of my total surrender to God. Because I was a self-sufficient, strong person, it was really hard to say, "I'm *not* in control." I wanted a guarantee. But in this moment, I *finally* began to let go.

Getting on the Road to Real Recovery

As our children grew, they had known to some degree that their dad had struggled, but they didn't really know any details. This time was different. After confessing to me, Steven decided to tell each of our children and their spouses, 12 people in all. He said, "I'm calling each one of our kids and telling them I need to meet with them tonight, separately."

It wasn't a big group meeting. He talked with one, then another, then another. His disclosing to our children, one by one, was an oddly healing and humbling experience for me. As I listened and watched him, I was especially pained to see and hear our children's reactions. Our two married sons each became red-faced and angry with their father. They each yelled, "How could you do that!?" In a roundabout way, I felt validation of my own feelings of betrayal and anger. It was healing in a strange way for me. Our three daughters cried and wanted to express their love, but felt so betrayed. With each of them, I wanted to calm them in some way, yet this was Steven's time to handle things.

As he told his story and asked each of our children for forgiveness, there was no minimization or justification on his part. His desire to be totally transparent, in spite of their reactions, showed his genuine humility. It was excruciating, but he did it anyway. He was willing to stay as long as was needed—no matter how painful. He answered their questions without reservation, and committed to each one that he would do whatever it would take to change his life.

In that painful setting, I began to see my husband as an honest, humbled, and accountable man. This recognition gave me a small glimpse of *what could be* if he chose to walk the path of recovery.

But I didn't know whether it would last. We were all hesitant to believe and trust immediately that healing and lasting change were on their way. Each of the children expressed a desire to see their dad really find true repentance. Even after they yelled and cried, each one said, "I hope you'll change, Dad."

With humility and honesty, Steven began to do whatever it took to work his recovery. I stood back. For months, I didn't get emotionally involved. I just watched what he would do; I was numb. I now took life in small degrees. I continually asked God whether I should leave, yet I received an answer to stay—at least for the moment.

At this writing, it is now seven years from that red letter fall Sunday morning when my husband disclosed his behavior to our children. His recovery continues to be miraculous. He has become a different man. Even his very countenance has changed. Yet I ask, what if *he* hadn't determined to change? *I* would still have needed my own recovery. *I* needed to become a different woman. I was not aware on that eventful day that *I* needed recovery from the trauma and betrayal that had occurred in my marriage and in my life. I once thought that if Steven recovered, our problems would be over. I have since learned that *my husband's recovery is not mine*. Each one of us comes to God individually, and the basis of recovery is a spiritual connection with God. I'm grateful my husband is working his recovery, but I will not fully heal without my own personal recovery.

From that day forward, I have chosen to find peace and joy one day at a time. Learning and growth take a lifetime. It's a process—not a six-week program, not an event. This is the rest of my story—or at least my progress until today. I don't have life all figured out; it's definitely not perfect. I won't have arrived, safely, until I'm safely dead.

Knowing I still have more ahead of me, I offer you these next chapters which contain the principles and lessons that have changed and continue to change my life. Peace, serenity, and even a measure of joy *are* available to you. *There is always hope.*

What I Can Do
Write your own story

YOU ARE NOT ALONE

It was a Sunday, several months after the third disclosure. I was feeling the pain of my husband's behaviors and addiction. As I sat with my family near the front of the chapel, I glanced at who was sitting in the pews behind and around us. My husband had been very active in our church; then all of a sudden he was released from his responsibilities and could not participate fully because of church discipline regarding his behavior. So I began to wonder who might recognize that he was not participating.

What could they be thinking about us? Other families looked happy, and here I was sitting with mine looking the same way. I worried that if they knew about our secret, they wouldn't accept us. *No one else is going through this*, I thought. *I've never heard of anybody in our community going through this.* I stewed about it for a few minutes and felt deep shame. Then I glanced over at my husband. He sat still, head bowed and eyes closed. There was a peaceful spirit about him. He didn't appear to be worrying about what people were thinking. I sensed that he was truly worshipping God. I closed my eyes and asked for the Lord's help to keep me focused on the Savior's love for me and for my husband. Still, I felt so completely alone in my pain.

I have wondered since that day how many women, perhaps even friends of mine, have suffered quietly—without support or understanding from anyone—as they have kept their grief to themselves and muscled through the pain on their own. Because there is so much shame and secrecy surrounding this topic, most, if not all, women—including me—experience feelings of extreme isolation. Yet we are all aware that pornography and sexual addictions are spreading throughout society like a pandemic. Statistics confirm that you are not the only one dealing with this issue—not even in your own neighborhood. Families everywhere are being confronted with the effects of pornography and sexual addictions. While its prevalence is distressing, it means that you are not alone.

No one can successfully handle this challenge alone. And thankfully, you do not need to.

The Isolating Effects of Shame

This particular addiction carries with it an enormous amount of shame, which in turn causes anyone involved to feel isolated. Other addictions do not seem to have the degree of shame that pornography and sexual addictions do. This addiction may be unique because of the high level of shame and secrecy that is attached to it. There is such a thing as "healthy guilt," which helps us to understand when we have done something wrong, and which encourages us to change. However, sexual addicts and their afflicted spouses often experience "toxic shame," a belief that they are flawed, unworthy, or bad people because of their behaviors.[2] This type of shame creates isolation, fear, hiding, minimizing, and a host of other unhealthy behaviors.

Due to shame, many doubt or won't acknowledge that addiction is in their home. Understanding the definition of *addiction,* and deciding whether addiction is truly in our home, will help us to connect to one another in our efforts to find support and recovery.

On a basic level, we define *sexual addiction* as a sexual behavior that has a negative effect on one's life. The four components that comprise addiction are 1) *compulsivity,* or feeling that one cannot stop the behavior after multiple attempts to stop; 2) *continuation,* or continuing the behavior despite negative consequences; 3) *preoccupation,* or thinking about the

---

[2] Dan Gray and Todd Olson, *"Addict Care Program,"* booklet, 4-5.

behavior, or about ways to participate in the behavior in the future; and 4) *tolerance*, or needing an increase of the same behavior, or an escalation to more intense behaviors to get the same "high." Others may define sexual addiction differently in an effort to minimize their behavior, but for us, this is a sound and comprehensive definition.

My own toxic shame caused me to wonder what was wrong with *me* for having chosen to marry someone with an addiction. Of course, at the time we married, I didn't know he was an addict, but I wondered why I hadn't been able to figure that out. So I questioned my ability to make wise choices. In my shame, I told myself that I was not attractive enough or experienced enough sexually to keep my husband's sexual interest. These feelings of toxic shame caused me to isolate.

In the recovery work I'm involved with now, I receive calls and emails nearly every day from women who have just discovered their husband's addiction; others have known there was something going on and have finally hit bottom in their lives. Usually it has taken months—if not years—for these women to finally reach out and tell someone what is going on in their family. I have felt that same isolation many, many times. Initially my husband did not want me to share the story of his behavior with others, but once I finally had the courage to talk to several trusted friends, I found much needed comfort and support.

A woman affected by pornography addiction in her marriage commented about shame, saying:

> *It was very difficult to let anyone in on the truth of my life. There was so much shame involved, which made me cover up and deny what was really going on. Shame, because I tried to blame myself; shame, because if I had been a better person we would be the happy family everyone thought we were.*[3]

Another woman expressed her concern that her family was the "freakiest" family in the community because they were dealing with this

---

3   Quoted from a personal conversation with the author. Sources for all such quotes throughout this book will not be provided in order to maintain confidentiality. Permissions have been obtained.

addiction. This is not the case; most families are in some way dealing with this problem.

Though your story may not be the same as mine, addiction is addiction, trauma is trauma, and recovery is recovery. Vast numbers of women are dealing with shame and therefore need recovery and connection.

For those dating someone with a sexual addiction, trauma is still present. Even women who are divorced from a sexual addict may be seeking for answers to their continued pain and confusion. Some may not know whether their ex-husband was a sexual addict until they learn what the red flags of addiction are, and what addict behavior looks like. Many of us, including myself, have never had any solid proof of our husband's betrayals, but with an understanding of the resultant behaviors—such as defensiveness, emotional disconnect, blame, secrecy, dishonesty, control, and other negative behaviors—we can begin to piece together the puzzle that has caused so much confusion, trauma, and shame in our lives.

Connection, Advocacy, and Validation

In order to find healing and recovery, we must dispel both isolation and shame. Dr. Jill Manning, a therapist who has long studied the effects of pornography and sexual addiction, found that *connection, advocacy,* and *validation* are critical for women who are in relationships with sexual addicts.[4] When I first read about this, I knew immediately that it fit for me. These three types of support are essential in dispelling shame and isolation. I hope my experience will direct women to similar resources.

Connection

Every woman who has had this affliction would be wise to make a *connection* with other women who have experienced feelings similar to theirs. Most of us have felt isolated. Sure, we can carry on a conversation sitting next to another mother at the soccer game or at a family gathering,

---

4   Jill C. Manning and Wendy L. Watson, "Common Factors in Christian Women's Preferences for Support When Dealing with a Spouse's Sexually Addictive or Compulsive Behaviors: The C.A.V.E.D. Theory," *Sexual Addiction & Compulsivity* 15, no. 3 (2008): 233-49, http://dx.doi.org/10.1080/10720160802288886.

but we may still feel totally alone. I have found meaningful connections in 12-Step support groups, and in a few trusted friends and family members.

Initially, I didn't feel the need to tell a lot of people. I chose my parents, who I knew would listen and love me and who also appreciated and loved my husband. You would do well to tell a few people, but they need to be trustworthy. They need to love you and your husband. They need to hold the information without becoming angry or judgmental. Telling someone who might gossip about you and your husband would not be wise. But be careful: you might feel tempted to tell others in revenge to punish him for his behavior, but that motivation is wrong. Be wise and patient on the when, how, and to whom you share such information. Be true to your best self in this.

One woman in recovery expressed:

> *I realized I had isolated myself and cut my support system down to nil. Part of this was because it felt so disloyal to discuss my husband's sins with anyone else. I dearly wanted to believe he was making good on his promises and didn't want to damage our relationship further by bringing others into it. Fortunately I had a close friend I already trusted who became my mentor after it became clear that she and I had some experiences in common. That, combined with recovery meetings and help from spiritual leaders, became a growing support system which I could trust to keep my experiences confidential.*

In addition to a connection with other people, I also needed a stronger connection to God to help me continue to have faith that *He* would strengthen me through the difficult days ahead. I found such a connection through soul-searching prayer, scripture study, and by looking to see God's hand in my life. Once I found a greater connection with both other women and God, I felt safe to begin my journey to recovery.

What Can I Do About ~~Him?~~ Me?

Advocacy

Sexual addicts have a difficult time respecting women because an addict's behavior leads them to use and objectify women regularly. I have also learned that individuals who are sexually addicted do not have the capacity to feel empathy for another's pain. So in order to feel safe, I needed an advocate, someone whom Steven would respect but who also could understand and validate my pain. Because I was not feeling safe in my marriage, I also needed someone with some degree of authority to work with my husband and me, and someone to hold him accountable for behaviors that were hurtful to me. But finding such people is not always easy.

After a lot of searching, I decided to choose from those who could advocate for my safety, such as a father, a spiritual leader, or a qualified sexual addiction therapist. You have to be honest with them about what is going on, and what *you* need. Be prayerful and wise about who you choose because they should be advocating for *your* safety, and for the safety of your family.

In time, I found the advocacy I sought in two individuals: in an educated, kind spiritual leader, and also in a qualified sexual addiction therapist. When you are looking for a qualified therapist, look for someone who understands sexual addictions, understands the wife's trauma and her need for healing, is clear about lifestyle changes needed to overcome the addiction, and can hold the addict accountable for his behaviors.

Validation

At each of my husband's disclosures to me, I experienced extreme feelings of self-doubt and fear. It took a long time for me to truly accept that my husband's behavior was not because of me or some perceived lack on my part. I had felt low self-esteem at times in my teen years, but thought I had overcome those negative feelings as a young adult. However, that insecurity came back with full force when I assumed that my husband's behavior was at least partially my fault. What I really needed was validation for my feelings of pain, trauma, and even anger.

One evening as I was leaving a recovery meeting with my husband, one of the therapists stopped us and said, "Rhyll, you have had more trauma in your life than most women." That surprised me. I had always felt that I had handled my pain in a positive way, and had simply tried to deal with it with my customary grit. But that comment caused me to deeply reflect. Even though I did not want to feel like a victim, I still needed to accept that I had indeed been victimized—and then deal with each of the attendant feelings. As I reflected, I realized that I had somewhat successfully buried these feelings for decades. But burying feelings is not dealing with them; it is merely hiding them. So I appreciated the validation I received in that comment, and in the years since, which have helped me to recognize my genuine feelings, and then learn to express them in an honest and direct, but not harmful, way.

There were times during this journey when I struggled to make even simple choices. For instance, I would go to the grocery store and feel like I was having a panic attack as I attempted to select basic items to keep feeding my family. I have since learned that this is typical for women who have been traumatized. Again, in these times, I needed someone to validate my pain. Thankfully, our qualified sexual addiction therapist, a 12-Step support program, and a strong, healthy sponsor empowered me to find strength. Through these outlets I have found validation in my pain and trauma, and have received encouragement to move forward as a survivor.

After Steven's third disclosure, we met with a qualified sexual addiction therapist. I was very doubtful that I could ever know when my husband was telling the truth, because for over 30 years, I discovered that I had not known. And I did not want to continue living in fear of constant betrayals. When I expressed my concerns and doubts about this, the therapist responded, "You will know." That simple statement planted in me a small seed of hope that I could indeed acquire the tools, inspiration, and courage to follow my gut in the future. So I slowed my life down. I read. I went to God and to other women who had experienced similar problems. The answers that I received were to take my time—at least a year—to work on my own healing, and see whether my husband was willing to find his recovery. That bit of validation and direction helped me to get to a point where I could again trust myself and trust God.

Moving Out Into the Light

As I began to work on my own recovery, I realized that I did not need to feel shame about myself or our situation. Once I understood and embraced that truth, I felt so much more peace. I no longer worried about what other people thought of me. While both my husband and I were working on solidifying our feelings regarding shame, we had a surprising and challenging opportunity to test our newfound confidence.

One afternoon in 2010, my cell phone rang. The woman on the other end introduced herself as a newspaper reporter and member of a committee that was developing an initiative called "Out in the Light." This media campaign was an effort to make people more aware of the serious nature of pornography, and the dire effect it has on women and relationships. She had heard that we had started a nonprofit foundation to benefit those who are sexually addicted, as well as their spouses, family members, and friends.

Then this reporter asked me a very direct question: "Why did you start your foundation?" I knew in that moment that I needed to give a very honest answer. So, taking a deep breath, I responded: "I am one of those women." We had not been public with our story before; at that time only our family and a few close friends knew. With this public disclosure, I was stepping into unknown territory, moving from the shadows of secrecy where these addictions trap so many. The reporter then asked if Steven and I would be willing to tell our story in the newspaper and in a television documentary. I told her that we would first have to prayerfully, thoughtfully, and carefully examine what that might mean to us as individuals, as a couple, and as a family.

Steven and I spent a couple of weeks in prayerful consideration. The subject of shame came to the forefront again. *What might our neighbors think? How might my husband's career be affected? What might they say at church about us?* These were scary prospects. We felt that our public disclosure could help so many, but it meant that our dirty laundry would be literally aired to the world.

After a lot of reflection, we agreed to the interview. We feel that much good has come from the information and experiences we have shared. Our desire to help alleviate some of the pain and wreckage in families diminished any hint of shame that surfaced. Nevertheless, we do not encourage other individuals or couples to indiscriminately share their experiences, but we do acknowledge that there needs to be more public discussion in order to start finding answers and healing for these vexing personal issues.

Sometime after the broadcast of our story, I was shopping at our local grocery store when I saw one of my friends from the neighborhood. We greeted each other warmly and went on with our shopping. About two minutes later, my friend came back down my aisle and stood quite close to me. She explained that she had heard our story and that she was very impressed with it. Then, moving even closer, she said in nearly a whisper, "Pornography is the reason my marriage ended." I was surprised to hear that, because she had told me previously that her divorce was due to an entirely different reason. About two weeks later, I saw another woman from our community whom I had not seen in at least a year. She came up to me, put her arms around me, and whispered, "Thank you for what you have shared. I am going through the same thing in my marriage right now." Their whispered secrets revealed the painful shame they had been enduring—alone. Both women had felt the need to share their pain with someone, and did so in very quiet tones to me.

It has been said that a pain shared is halved;
a joy shared is doubled.

There are hundreds and thousands of women today who may feel isolated, sad, and hopeless. A high percentage of families struggle with pornography and sexual addiction in some way, and the numbers increase daily. Learning to be appropriately open and honest will help not only ourselves but also many, many others who feel so much shame and isolation because of this problem. There are many women, including myself, who are committed to reach out and share our experience and our hope—hope for peaceful and even joyful lives in spite of our trauma because of someone else's behavior.

You are not alone in this. You are unique but your situation is not. Though we will each need to find our own path, our needs are much the same, and together—and with God's help—we can meet our challenges with courage and strength. You won't need to look far to find someone who understands what you're going through. Then, with recovery, you too can stand as a friend ready to give encouragement, confidence, strength, and spiritual direction to another in need. *You* are not alone. *We* are not alone.

What I Can Do

CHOICES

I have made a lot of "mistakes" in this journey. I hesitate to use the word *mistake* because each choice I made was part of my life's experience and an opportunity for learning; likewise, each choice you have made is part of your path. The goal is to do a little better each day, based on new knowledge we may have acquired. So I guess all the mistakes I have made are why I can say, with humility, *I am thoroughly qualified to talk and write about this subject.*

Twenty-five years ago, when my husband first disclosed his betrayals to me, I chose to feel partly responsible for his addiction. I felt then that I was part of the problem. My personal journal entries from those years are replete with the phrase, "If only I can be better, then everything will be okay." I thought that if I were more loving and more attentive, Steven would change. So I would leave love notes in his suitcase and on his pillow, hoping that would discourage him from acting out. When comparing myself to the images he was looking at, I felt inadequate physically. So I thought that if I were just more sexual, I could catch and hold his attention. If I were smarter, he would admire me more.

I tried harder and harder to be more attractive to him and to improve myself in his eyes. Still, his emotionally disconnected behavior toward me continued for years. When I asked how he was doing, he always assured me that he was doing just fine. And I really wanted to believe him. When he said *he* was doing okay, I then though that *I* must be the crazy one. So I tried to avoid the problem by making it about me. By making the problem about *me*, I was actually enabling *his* behavior. That was my first mistake.

After nearly ten years of believing that I was part of the problem, my husband came forward with his second disclosure. Again he was sad, remorseful, and said he wanted to change. He confessed that he did not know how to deal with this. There just seemed to be no meaningful answers for him. I finally shifted, and began to realize that I had not caused his problem. Interestingly, I went into rescuer mode. I bought into the idea that since he could not help himself, it was up to me to carry him along—to fix it for him. That was my second mistake.

For a time, it appeared that I was doing the right thing in finding help for him and being so supportive. The few people who were aware expressed admiration for my rescuing efforts, which only encouraged me the more. I felt fulfilled, and found great purpose to my life in "carrying" my husband. (Only later, when we had found the proper tools and were seriously working our own recovery, did my husband share how deeply he had resented me during those years. I could hardly believe his ingratitude for all the sacrifices I had made! I played the martyr role quite well. But to repeat, by not allowing him to find recovery for himself, I had enabled his weaknesses.)

More years passed, and then came the third disclosure. I felt like my marriage was now over. None of my efforts to blame myself, to try harder, to threaten divorce, or to carry him along had worked. I finally began to embrace the truth that because I did not cause my husband's addiction, I could not fix it for him—and I could not control the outcome. I knew then that there was only one place left for me to go to find the answer. I went to God.

This time, I went in total surrender to His will. I had been asking God for guidance from the moment I first met Steven, but I had always followed my own will in an effort to control the outcome. But now, if I was going to leave my husband I was determined to find out whether it was truly God's will. I had to be in a place where I was connected with God so that I could be sensitive to where He was directing me.

I looked for that answer to leave. Yet it did not come the first day, or the first week, or even the first month after his third disclosure. A qualified sexual addiction therapist suggested that I not throw him out—just yet. I was advised to learn what recovery was, and determine whether my husband was willing to do what it takes to be in recovery.

Today, I am grateful that I continue to take time to find my own healing, and that I've been able to see a meaningful transformation in my husband. Because I changed, my life changed. And he changed. On his own, Steven resolved to change his own behavior and work his own recovery with the help of God, education, a qualified therapist, and a 12-Step support group—with or without me. That is what recovery requires: total submission to God's will and complete trust in His plan.

A Bit About Sexual Addiction

To make an educated decision about the future of our relationships, we need to understand certain key aspects about addiction, sobriety, and recovery. First, *sobriety* is not the same as *recovery*. Sexual *sobriety* is "no form of sex with self or anyone else other than a spouse of the opposite sex, and includes progressive victory over lust."[5] My husband and I believe that viewing pornography crosses the boundary of sobriety as well. My husband could go for years in a state of sobriety without being in recovery. *Recovery* requires both "a life style change and a change of heart."[6] Furthermore,

> *[recovery] includes recognizing and admitting to being an addict, setting appropriate boundaries to protect against future acting out, learning to cope with life in healthy and appropriate ways, being willing to work on recovery daily, and changing the underlying behaviors that cause the individual to seek out pornography.*[7]

---

5   Sexaholics Anonymous, *White Book* (N.p: Sexaholics Anonymous, 1989), 191-92.
6   S. A. Lifeline Foundation, *Understanding Pornography and Sexual Addiction: A Resource for LDS Families and Leaders* (San Antonio: Forward Press Publishing, 2011), 42.
7   Ibid

What Can I Do About ~~Him?~~ *Me?*

It is also important to understand addict behaviors and actions, and recovery behaviors and actions. What is the difference? I would say that *actions* are a state of doing, whereas *behaviors* are a state of being.

For example, *addict actions* include acting out sexually by viewing pornography, masturbating, and engaging in any other sexual relationship outside of the marital relationship. *Addict behaviors* include being dishonest, acting like a victim, being emotionally disconnected, hiding, being easily angered, minimizing, denying, blaming, and showing a lack of empathy. We don't often attribute these behaviors to addiction, but when someone is in true recovery these behaviors disappear. So when these behaviors are still present, the addict is not in recovery.

On the other hand, *recovery actions* include attending 12-Step meetings, going to therapy, working the steps, and reading about recovery. *Recovery behaviors* include being honest, being respectful, showing kindness, and being accountable, patient, and emotionally available. As we gain a better sense of addict behaviors and actions and recovery behaviors and actions, we are better able to see where we—and our husbands—are in our recovery journey. Using these principles, we are in a better place to make wise choices.

Having made many mistakes, I can look back now and understand that the key to making wise choices, whatever our situation may be, is becoming educated, taking some time, and asking specifically for and relying on inspiration from God.

Four Options

In my associations, I have seen women make several different choices as wives of sexual addicts. The following are options, and every woman will have to decide for herself by considering her situation and her family status. My hope is that each of us will make a decision that is firmly rooted in prayer and education about the issues we are dealing with. Keeping that in mind, let's explore four choices that are open to us.

1. Throw Him Out

One obvious option is to throw him out on his ear. We have the opportunity to say, "You're out of here or I'm out of here. I'm done. I'm packing my bags, taking the kids, and filing for divorce." That's one possibility. This might be a natural response to a husband's traumatizing betrayal, especially when that behavior has escalated (as it nearly always does because of the nature of addiction) from "just pornography" to strip clubs, prostitution, affairs, or any number of more heinous behaviors. If the decision to divorce is made with great prayer, education, and counsel, it can be a positive choice.

But I must be candid here. There were plenty of times when I just wanted to be rid of the pain and thought that I should leave—or mostly wished that *he* would leave. I think I understand why this choice seems appealing and even logical. Yet one potential consequence of that decision is that if I choose to make it all about *him* and *his* behavior, and I leave, I may lose the opportunity to look at *myself* and discover why *I* made that choice in the first place, and why I continue to feel so betrayed and traumatized.

Years ago, I feared the possibility of my entire marriage falling apart. I worried that I would not have the financial security that my family would need to survive. That fear faded as I gained self-confidence and turned to God with full purpose of heart. I knew that whatever happened could be tough, but also that we could manage.

There were also times when I believed that the grass might be greener somewhere else. However, there is a very high likelihood that if I were to divorce without finding recovery, and chose to marry again, I would go into another marriage with the same type of man. Grim as this sounds, the percentages are not in favor of finding a man who does not have the same problems. Even if I did marry a man without these challenges, without taking care of my own recovery, I would not have the healing, peace, and confidence needed to be happy in a new relationship.

Now I must say right here that if a husband and father is abusive physically, sexually, or emotionally, we must keep ourselves and our children safe. Some may try to minimize their husband's sexual demands or aggressive behaviors, but the husband's behaviors still constitute abuse. In this case, and with the support of our chosen advocate, either we must require the husband to remove himself from the home, or we must leave with the children to a safe place until we are confident that there is safety. In abusive situations, decisive action is required immediately.

Even in these instances, though, it is possible to find recovery. A separation does not necessarily mean a foot in the divorce door. Once you are out of immediate danger, a qualified sexual addiction therapist can help a woman make important decisions for her case. The decisions of divorce should be prayerfully made and inspired by God.

Regardless of my choice, it is my personal recovery that gives me the tools to develop a closer connection with God, and the confidence to follow my gut instincts. Personal recovery, independent of my decision to stay or go, blesses my life in every way.

2. *Persecutor*

Some women choose to make life as miserable for their husbands as possible to punish them for their unsavory behavior. That is the *persecutor* option. These women seem to think that being mean or punishing will help them get revenge and make them feel better. They might even feel they are bringing justice to the situation. I know well those feelings of anger; however, I know that staying in that angry place—being mean and trying to make my husband pay for the pain he has caused me—is contrary to the best that can be me. This doesn't mark the kind of person I want to be, nor is it a fitting use of all that is good in me.

It's important to work through those raw feelings constructively with someone who can help us find a positive outcome. Even though you may feel victimized by somebody's behavior, staying angry and punishing that person will only canker your soul. My husband has been a sick person—not a bad person who has chosen to be mean or punish me. Even when it felt like it was directed at me, it was not.

3. Police Woman

Another option is for us to take responsibility for his addiction by saying, "He *is* feeling sad and remorseful. He wants to clean up, but I'm sure he can't do it without me. He needs me to help him by policing the computer. He wants me to tell him at the end of the week whether he's been good or bad." The *police woman* checking the computer history, texts, phone bills, glove boxes, and pants pockets will nearly always feel anxious. She may drive around looking for his car at strip clubs or adult stores. She lives in almost constant fear. If she doesn't do her job well enough and control it and control him, she just knows that he's going to act out again.

This type of behavior is understandable. We don't want to be duped or lied to again, and so we are hypervigilant to keep ourselves safe from further betrayal. While this may be a step towards finding safety, we must eventually move into a true recovery. Until we have acquired some genuine trust in ourselves through our own recovery process, we will likely continue to feel high anxiety and craziness.

This is also what I call the *crazy committee*! That's the term I use for the way my brain has responded over the years to fear: if I don't control everything, my life will fall apart. I've heard it said that when you're in your own head, you're behind enemy lines. Not one of us has the capacity to control someone else's behavior, but still we try, try, try. That is the core of the police woman's attitude.

For example, there are women who monitor their husband's computers constantly, or check the phone bill monthly. I have even heard of women who require their husband, when he is traveling, to take the TV remote to the front desk of the hotel and give it to the hotel clerk. Then the clerk must tell the wife on the husband's cell phone that he has given over the remote. These inappropriate behaviors heighten fear and anxiety in us as women, and encourage further shame and resentment in the husbands. Even now, if I am in a mind-set of fear, I may worry if my husband doesn't pick up his cell phone that he might be looking for a prostitute. In those moments, however, I try to choose peace and serenity instead—working my own recovery, and surrendering the responsibility for his behavior to him.

What Can I Do About ~~Him?~~ Me?

4. Recovery

Early on in my husband's recovery I thought, *What can I do about him? If somebody could just fix him, then all my problems would be gone.* His behavior was a really convenient place to put blame for a multitude of my problems. For instance, if the kids were misbehaving, it was because he had not been an active father! If our finances were totally out of control, it was because of his addiction! And the list went on. Yet each of these accusations was not entirely true. Certainly, the addiction did create severe havoc in our lives, but I needed to take a deeper look at *myself* and say, *What can I do about me? Is the way I am reacting to this situation healthy?* I needed to ask this, not in any effort to try to change my husband's behavior, but in recognition that I haven't arrived at perfection either.

I'm not a sex addict, but I do recognize a need to improve myself in other areas. Yet to me, my husband's behaviors were "big sins" and my own imperfections of being judgmental and self-righteous were a lot further down the ladder in comparison. Because I had tried very hard in my life to do what I believed was right, I concluded that if I was judgmental, then I certainly had good reason to be! This is justification; instead of recognizing in humility that my prideful, judgmental, blaming behavior was a sin, I mistakenly called evil good.

> *Lord, help me to be patient with those*
> *who sin differently than I.*

This principle may be tricky for people who have been betrayed and deeply traumatized by someone else's actions. Understanding that we all have attributes and behaviors that we need to improve does not diminish or disregard our pain; rather, that understanding encourages us to stretch so that we can feel true to our best selves. So as I change the way I react, the family dynamics can change for the better. Something will change—but not until *I* change.

> *If we would change the world, we must first move ourselves.*
> — Ghandi

I've become aware of my own need for change through the 12-Step program. Part of the program required me to make a list of my character defects. This exercise was quite painful. It required a lot of humility and deep digging. So I started listing my character assets and discovered that some of my character assets were also defects when taken to an extreme. For instance, I have prided myself in being responsible. But being *too* responsible took me into control-and-fix mode. My husband used to ask me what I wanted for Christmas, and I'd reply, "An honest husband." I wanted my husband to be honest, humble, and accountable, but I didn't realize that I needed to hold myself to that same standard of honesty, humility, and accountability. I needed to acknowledge my own faults, and trust that God can take my defects and strengthen me if I willingly give them up to Him. However difficult, that's a blessing!

What if I choose not to work my own recovery? It is certainly an option, and I can choose that option. Many of us who go through this trauma are unwilling to look at ourselves and acknowledge that, as imperfect human beings, we have character traits that we can improve. Not working on our own recovery may leave us thinking that our problems are all his fault!

What is frightening and concerning to me about this principle is that if we do not learn how to become healthy and recover, we will likely make the same mistakes over and over. We will tend to attract the same kind of people. If I'm a rescuer—someone who enjoys taking care of and rescuing other people who need my help, then I will likely—although sub-consciously—find someone else who needs rescuing. And with the prevalence of sexual addiction, I'm likely to find another sexual addict who needs "fixing." What is sad is how many women have been married to two, three, or even five sexual addicts. These women have not changed—and so their circumstances have not changed.

Women working their recovery, on the other hand, begin to understand themselves better. They learn that whatever the outcome of their marriage, they can choose to be healthy and find a measure of joy. Recovery requires work. It takes time to attend our support groups, call our sponsors, and become humble, honest, and accountable in all areas of our lives. But we find that our self-confidence increases and our ability to keep ourselves safe by setting appropriate boundaries gives us more courage and hope for the future.

After a presentation a woman came up to me and said, "You seem to be happy. How can that be after all you've been through?" I was surprised! I was surprised because I *am* happy! I asked myself, *How is it that I am happy?* I realized that it was because of three things: my recognition of God's love, my own efforts in recovery, and the support of so many who understand. Through this I have peace in my life—even joy and happiness.

Granted, there are still difficulties: *Will we make the house payment? Who will my son marry? Do I spend enough time with my grandchildren? Am I taking on too much of other people's recovery? Will the addict behaviors return?* and so on. But I've realized that wading through the difficulties of this affliction has taken me to a place of trust in God that I've never experienced before. There's self-confidence and courage too, but the very center is trust in God.

I choose recovery one day at a time, and I encourage every woman to do the same. I hope all will join me in recognizing that through this affliction, we have an opportunity to find great healing, peace, and connection with God. As I find all of those positives in my life, there will be light in me that will attract other light. If my husband chooses not to work his own recovery, and returns to lies and betrayal, he will move toward the dark and away from the light. On the other hand, if he chooses to become honest, humble, and accountable, there will be light in him and in his life. Either way, and no matter what choice he makes, I can be happy, because my recovery leads me to happiness and light.

I recognize that this may not be the sweet, wonderful message you want to hear. This is a hard, "I have work to do" message. For years, I didn't want to hear it myself. You may read this entire book and not be ready for it. I understand that we all have our own path. But please accept that this message of recovery is the one that will bring you lasting hope and healing, and I'm offering it to you from my heart.

What I Can Do

PART TWO

Working on Me

NO WAY BUT THROUGH

In the summertime, Cache Valley, Utah, is a gloriously green area with beautiful vistas at every turn. In the dead of winter, however, those turns become treacherous, icy, and threatening. Late one night many years ago during one such winter, I was driving home with my children when the fog became really dense—so dense that I couldn't see the road. There wasn't any way I could stop on this two-lane highway without someone running into us from behind, and I was terrified of driving into the icy water that lined each side of the road. The horrifying thought went through my mind, "How can I rescue my children from a sinking car?" As I inched along the highway, I clenched the steering wheel with one hand and used the other to hold open the van door so that I could see the line down the middle of the road. I said to my kids, "Just keep praying that we get home safely." As I slowly continued on, I kept my door open, looking for and following that white line. It took us a long time to finally reach the safety of home.

Looking back, I realize how that experience relates to my recovery process. It was hard for me to imagine an end to all the hurt, the trauma, the betrayal, and the hopelessness; all I wanted to do was to get home safely; all I could do was survive from one minute to the next.

Recovering from the trauma of a spouse's sexual addiction is a painful and slow process. As afflicted spouses, we have literally been traumatized.

This is what researchers call an *attachment trauma*. Geoff Steurer, a marriage and family therapist, said:

> *Many scholars have noted that women betrayed by their husband's pornography use experience symptoms associated with post-traumatic stress disorder, a condition that is equated with feelings of powerlessness, intrusive thoughts and memories, and efforts to avoid the triggers associated with the traumatic stressor.*[8]

He further writes:

> *Shock, denial, anger, rage, depression, self-loathing, isolation, and fear are some of the words that describe what a woman experiences when she learns of her husband's secretive sexual behaviors. Virtually every woman I've worked with has experienced deep shame, embarrassment, and humiliation.*[9]

Upon learning of a spouse's betrayal, we can expect to experience this form of trauma; this is the rule and not the exception.

One woman explained her trauma in this way:

> *Hearing my husband disclose his sexual addiction behaviors…was like I was watching the cars pile up in a horrendous train wreck. It felt like being in a war zone with no safety in sight. Every memory I had was tainted by the new information I had been given. Every concept of who my husband was and what our family was seemed to explode anew with each newly recognized betrayal. It hurt like hell to have to acknowledge to myself over and over again that the man I thought would die to protect me and*

---

[8] Geoff Steurer, "What's A Woman to Do? How Pornography Affects Women and What They Can Do," *Geoff Steurer: Licensed Marriage and Family Therapist* (blog), September 20, 2010, http://www.geoffsteurer.com/archives/377.

[9] Ibid.

my kids had in fact [driven] head on into us, with his foot firmly on the gas.

Becoming aware of such disloyalty is deeply painful, and we should not consider ourselves weak, sinful, or unwise when we feel devastated and angry by our husbands' sexually acting out; nevertheless, we have to trudge our way through and past those feelings. That is the only way.

Be Where Your Feet Are

One of the best pieces of advice I've ever received was to frequently ask myself, *How is your life right now in this very moment?* Over time, and throughout the heartache, I've learned *not* to ask, *What's going to happen tomorrow?* or even *What do I need to do in an hour?* Instead, I've learned to think, *How am I right now? What do I feel around me at this very moment?* Sometimes I feel warmth and peace, and sometimes I feel heartache and pain. I try to enjoy the beauty of a flower, the beaming rays of the sun, or the majesty of the mountains around me. It is purposeful to recognize how I feel in the moment, whether it is sadness, happiness, loneliness, or joy.

As I pay more attention to the present moment, I better see God's blessings, and the proof that He knows me and cares about me. Part of what I've discovered for myself, and what I want to share with other women, is how to see in the present moment evidence that God loves each one of us. I've come to find peace in His love. I cannot control what's going to happen tomorrow—nobody can. But as we choose to live in the present moment, we can find peace and serenity amidst our afflictions. I choose to live in the present moment. I choose to be where my feet are.

Recovery Is a Process

Recovery is a *process*; it is not an *event*. We are part of a quick fix generation; we just want to get things done. I have heard women on the phone and in recovery meetings say, "I want to be done with this pain. I want to be done with the whole thing. Do you have a six-week program?"

No, this will not take six weeks. It will become a lifelong journey of constant learning. I would have missed the progress and growth I needed in my life if my recovery had consisted of a six-week program. Recovery is not a short-term process because recovery means continually cultivating a healthier lifestyle of peace.

One woman in recovery stated:

> *In this messy business of recovery, I am sure I will fall flat in the mud many times more. I am sure I will struggle for breath and cry for relief. I bet I even have a few more absolute crisis moments waiting for me on this road, but now, today at least, I am willing to walk it anyway. One step at a time, one moment at a time. I am willing because I have discovered that I am not bound to follow in my husband's self-destructive path.*

Another woman in recovery articulated this principle perfectly. She said:

> *It takes as long as it takes. Grieving—whether it is from death, divorce, or perhaps the death of one's dreams—cannot be rushed. Forgiveness cannot be rushed. Healing cannot be rushed. I adopted the attitude, "I am willing to do my part to heal, I am willing to forgive, I am willing to work on myself, and I will trust my Higher Power to help make the miracles happen. I will not be dishonest by claiming my forgiveness is complete. I will not lie to myself by saying my healing is achieved. Instead, I will surrender to the process and welcome the healing as it comes.*

Others have commented that not living in the present has caused them fear and anxiety. We should look to the past only to learn, and look to the future only to plan.

Pain Is the Pathway to Progress

Not only is the pain of recovery a process, it is a transformative process. We are being refined as God "makes our heart as gold."[10] One of my favorite quotes reads:

> *Imagine yourself as a living house. God comes in to rebuild that house. At first, perhaps, you can understand what He is doing. He is getting the drains right and stopping the leaks in the roof and so on; you knew that those jobs needed doing and so you are not surprised. But presently He starts knocking the house about in a way that hurts abominably and does not seem to make any sense.*
>
> *What on earth is He up to? The explanation is that He is building quite a different house from the one you thought of—throwing out a new wing here, putting on an extra floor there, running up towers, making courtyards. You thought you were being made into a decent little cottage: but He is building a palace. He intends to come and live in it Himself.*[11]

God is doing things in our lives that sometimes hurt abominably. They are very painful. Yet what He is doing is transforming us from average women to exceptional women. The process is not easy, and it's certainly not comfortable, but it is worth it. What this process will do is refine us—whatever challenge we go through. It is essential for us to understand that pain is often the pathway to progress.

None of us want pain. Even worse than feeling our own pain is seeing our children or loved ones in pain. I remember being in the hospital room when one of our daughters had a miscarriage and hemorrhaged. She was losing much blood and crying out in pain. Her face turned white and tears rolled down her cheeks right before she fainted. The doctors rushed her into

---

10 Roger Hoffman, *Consider the Lilies: Vocal Solo* (Orem, Utah: Jackman Music Corporation, 1986), 5-6.
11 C. S. Lewis, *Mere Christianity* (New York: Harper Collins, 2001), 205.

the ER, away from me and her husband. I felt pangs of terror thinking about the kind of agony she must be in. I wished that I could take away her pain.

As mothers and as women, we do not like to see people hurting. Yet when I look at my own life, I realize that my kind, loving Heavenly Father knows I'm going to experience pain—and He allows it to happen. He knows that pain and struggle will bring me closer to Him in humility.

I have had moments when I was drawn to my knees because of my emotional pain, sobbing and pleading for His comfort. I have bloodied my knuckles at heaven's door. I admit that if I had never grappled with that agony, I never would have prayed for comfort or recognized what great peace God has to offer me. Through such experiences, I was making headway and learning to rely upon the Lord.

Realizing that these principles benefit myself, should I shield opportunities for growth from my loved ones? I am reminded of the story of the Prodigal Son in Luke 15. I doubt that the father in the story hoped his son would encounter so much difficulty. And yet it was the adversity the son experienced that eventually brought him back home. Just like the father in the parable, as parents and spouses we may pray that something will come into the life of our loved one who is making bad choices that will cause him to change. I faithfully prayed for years and years for my husband to "come to himself," as did the Prodigal Son. I just didn't know exactly how it might happen.

When my husband was arrested for soliciting a prostitute, our family was traumatized all over again. My children were furious and devastated, and I was in shock. My husband felt utterly humiliated. But it was the very torment he needed to interrupt his course in life. As he says in his own story, that experience was so traumatizing to him that he finally realized how out of control his life was. He now sees that torment, that interruption, as a gift from God. In retrospect, he contends that the arresting officers in their blue uniforms were actually angels who were sent to declare, "This is your opportunity."

How many of us as mothers and wives have the courage to allow our spouses or children to face the consequences of their own actions—and be blessed by the potential growth? What if I had stood in the way of that?

What if I had minimized the effect his behaviors had on our family by choosing to sweep everything under the rug? I would have swept away opportunity for growth.

When we look into the future, we may fear that we can't possibly overcome our most difficult challenges, but those challenges are exactly what we need. We should not opt out of such experiences in our lives; we should keep going forward. And with God's loving care, He will get us through them—not just to survive, but to emerge triumphantly. We will find that we are more than we were when we began.

Even now, I occasionally go to a "poor me" place for a moment or two and will say, *I just want a normal life.* Then I think, *Wait, what is a normal life?* I then recognize that there is no such thing as normal. I also think, *Would I go back to what I thought was my normal life 25 years ago, before I really knew what addiction was about and what recovery took?* Would I go back? *Never!* I would never go back to that life because my life has improved through the refining fire of difficulty and pain.

Are there still tough days? Yes. But I have been blessed with the opportunity to find recovery and peace through this affliction. My marriage is healthier, and we are more intimately connected. The bar has been raised for us. We no longer are content with a parallel relationship; we are working towards a unified, synergistic relationship that I did not know was even possible. How grateful I am! You can't experience the joy unless you have felt the pain—and we have been there.

For those who consistently seek and live the principles of recovery, the fog *will* lift. Some days, I drive down that same road in Cache Valley; where once there was the darkness of fog, I often find beautiful sunshine. Instead of creeping slowly down the road watching the middle white line, I am flying down the road with the wind blowing through my hair! The scenery can change and has changed in my life. Getting through doesn't always mean it will be dense and difficult and slow going, but it does mean that no matter what circumstances we are in, we should keep moving on that road. There is no way but through.

What I Can Do

BOUNDARIES:
THE MOST LOVING THING I CAN DO

One summer while we (were still) living on our farm, our son had a 4-H project of raising a steer for the fall county fair. The kids named him "Bruiser" because he was a large and menacing-looking animal. We kept him fenced in the pasture next to the road that ran in front of our home. One afternoon Bruiser became agitated. He ran around the pasture and eventually ran straight at the fence, crashing through it and across the road. That fence was a boundary. It kept Bruiser where we knew he was safe and where he wouldn't harm other people and property. When he crossed this boundary, there was no telling where the destruction would end.

A boundary is simply "any line or thing marking a limit."[12] Setting boundaries gives us real power over the chaos surrounding sexual addiction and addict behaviors. Just as Bruiser required boundaries for his safety and the safety of others, boundaries in our relationships are also for safety. When we don't have boundaries, we may allow ourselves to be manipulated. Boundaries can nurture emotional energy and help us develop wisdom and self-respect. Establishing and maintaining boundaries is one way we show love for others and for ourselves.

---

12   *Webster's New World Dictionary,* 2nd ed., s.v. "Boundary."

What Can I Do About ~~Him?~~ Me?

Setting Boundaries

Boundaries may be an entirely new concept for most women who are suffering through this affliction. In recovery meetings, it's common to hear women say things such as, "I had no idea I could set boundaries; I didn't know I could set limits for myself." For me, the concept of boundaries was a pivotal lesson in my recovery; I suddenly had permission to be myself.

But who was I? I had lost myself, and I had to work on finding me before I could set my boundaries. In the past, my husband would say, "Where do you want to go to eat?" and I'd say, "I don't know; wherever you want." I thought I had to concede to what everybody else wanted, and somehow that made me a better person. I thought I didn't deserve to have my own needs or wants! I didn't know whether my needs and wants mattered. I didn't realize I could have boundaries.

Learning for myself, and then expressing my needs, wants, and values to my husband, was an essential prerequisite to setting appropriate boundaries. But merely clarifying and expressing my wishes is not truly setting a boundary. A boundary should empower you and give you a sense of choice by providing you with a plan of action. This plan of action can be found in an "If-Then" statement. The "If…" is the boundary; the "Then…" is the plan of action.

Boundaries can be relatively small and insignificant, such as "If I get tired in the middle of the day, then I will rest." They can also be large and significant, and have life-changing consequences: "If I feel manipulated and verbally abused, then I will not answer your phone calls or emails;" or, "if you want to talk about our separation, then make an appointment with our therapist."

Some boundaries may be obvious and basic: "I will not allow any pornography or acting out sexually in our home; so if you bring pornography or acting out into our home, then we will need to be separated for a time so I can work on my recovery." Others may be more personal and specific to our unique needs: "If I am tempted to look online for another extreme diet, then I will instead call my sponsor to talk about why I am feeling physically inadequate again."

After setting a boundary, everything the addict does will be feedback and indicate how you are to proceed. When he chooses to ignore your boundary, what then? You will know what to do based on how the boundary was set. Your plan of action is inherent in the boundary (If..., then...). It is time for you to carry out the "then...."

After setting a boundary, it can be easy to cave in, or minimize his actions because of our own fears. However, if we abandon the boundary and don't carry out the consequences, we diminish our power and feel much less secure.

Examples of How Boundaries Can Change Your Life

In relationships with others and with ourselves, there are at least six types of boundaries: mental, emotional, physical, spiritual, financial, and sexual. The book *Lord, I Believe; Help Thou Mine Unbelief* by Rod Jeppsen, a licensed professional counselor and sexual addictions therapist, provides examples of specific boundaries within these six categories.

Example 1: Mental Boundaries
Before Boundaries Were Set

Husband: *I'm going to vote for Mr. Hansen for the city council. I know him personally and think he would be the very best choice.*

Wife: *I think I will too!*

Notice how she agrees with her husband without even considering what she really thinks or intends to do. Let's assume she has had reservations about voting for Mr. Hansen, but did not say anything to her husband about her concerns. Without boundaries, she has become enmeshed with her husband's thinking, and no longer thinks for herself. Over time, this wife has been manipulated and feels that her thoughts or opinions do not matter, so she just goes along with her husband. She has not set a mental boundary for herself, or decided to say "yes" to her own opinions and thoughts, and be responsible for them. She may not realize she can say "no," or she may be afraid to say "no" to her husband's opinion and vote for the candidate of her choice. Yet she needs to give herself that right; she has that choice. She has the right to be an equal, and to share her own thoughts and feelings.

Here is an example of the same conversation where the wife uses her agency, has set her own mental boundary, and respectfully expresses her own thoughts and opinions:

After Boundaries Were in Place

Husband: *I'm going to vote for Mr. Hansen for the city council. I know him personally and think he would be the very best choice.*

Wife: *I'm not sure yet how I will cast my vote. I have read a lot of information concerning each candidate, and right now I am actually leaning toward Mr. Jensen.*

Example 2: Emotional Boundaries
Before Boundaries Were Set

Husband: *You are never interested in sex.*

Wife: *That's not true, I am interested in sex—just not as often as you.*

Husband: *Well, you never initiate sex, and I can't remember the last time you appeared to be interested—probably on our honeymoon."* (Husband is upset and keeps adding more digs to extend the argument.)

Wife: *I've been interested in sex lots of times; you just don't choose to remember any of them!*

Without an emotional boundary in place, the wife allows herself to get emotionally charged up, defends herself, counterattacks, and continues to argue with her husband about their sexual intimacy.

Compare the same discussion after emotional boundaries were set, where the wife decides she will no longer argue with her husband about the frequency of sexual intimacy, nor go through the emotional trauma each time he brings up the subject.

After Boundaries Were in Place

Husband: *You are never interested in sex.*

Wife: *There are times when physically, mentally, or emotionally I prefer not to engage in sexual intimacy.* (Wife focuses on her own feelings rather than on what he said, and shares these feelings with her husband.)

Husband: *Well, you never initiate sex, and I can't remember the last time you appeared to be interested—probably on our honeymoon.* (Husband is upset and keeps adding more digs to extend the argument.)

Wife: *I'm sorry you feel the way you do, and I sense that you are getting upset about this. I'm more than willing to discuss our sexual intimacy, but I choose not to argue about it. You can either lower your voice so we can talk civilly to each other, or I will end the conversation. What would you prefer?*

Notice that with an emotional boundary in place, the wife now knows exactly where she will end the conversation. She should be kind and avoid verbally attacking her husband, but she can still make clear what her limits are. In the second series, the wife has set an emotional boundary for herself that she will no longer argue about sexual intimacy, and become angry. When we pre-set emotional boundaries, we are less likely to buy into or be manipulated by our loved ones' arguments or accusations, and become emotionally upset in the process.

More than likely, our loved ones will not like our new response. In fact, they may say things that are hurtful and mean to bait us back into the argument. They know what has worked in the past to manipulate us, and they will not easily give up using these methods. We can respect our spouse's viewpoint, even though we do not agree with it. He is entitled to his viewpoint and we are entitled to ours; we determine what our boundaries are in regard to sharing those viewpoints.

Example 3: Physical Boundaries
Before Boundaries Were Set

Husband: *You are making such a big deal out of nothing. So what if I view pictures of naked women on the computer? National Geographic magazines show naked women too.*

Wife: *I don't think it is a good idea to be looking at naked women."*

Husband: *Like I say, you are blowing something so minor into this huge problem.* (Husband's voice is raised and his body language shows he is becoming angry.)

Wife: *Well fine, let's not talk about it anymore.*

Without physical boundaries, the wife began questioning herself, and wondered if maybe she was indeed blowing this matter out of proportion. Because she had not set a clear boundary, she backpedaled on her position and compromised her own ethics and values about having no pornography in the home. She also seems to take responsibility for her husband's anger. In the process, she was losing her own identity—what she stands for—and was becoming enmeshed with her husband. She was almost dissolving herself by accepting his position on pornography, even though deep down she knew it was wrong.

After Boundaries Were in Place

Here is a simplified dialogue between a husband and wife where the wife has set a firm boundary about no pornography in the home:

Husband: *You are making such a big deal out of nothing. So what if I view pictures of naked women on the computer? National Geographic magazines show naked women too.*

Wife: *This is a very important issue for me and for our children. I will not accept any pornography in our home.*

Husband: *Like I say, you are blowing something that is so minor into this huge problem.* (Husband's voice is raised and his body language shows he is becoming angry.)

Wife: *I'm sorry that you seem to be angry about this, but it is not right to bring pornography into our home, affecting the children and me. So if you bring Internet pornography into our home, I will install a filter and password on the computer. I do not want pornography from any source in our home.*

By setting boundaries and sticking with them, we cultivate inner strength, and recognize that we do have the right and the ability to take a stand. We also realize that we are not helpless in this matter, and that there are many options from which to choose.

In the second series, the wife had set clear boundaries on what she expected in the home. She was firm and direct with her comments to her husband. She acknowledged that he was angry, and mentioned that she was sorry that he felt that way. However, she also recognized that she is not responsible for his anger; he is responsible for his own anger. Her husband's anger, directed at her boundaries, is not a reason for her to change them. By setting boundaries, she has not taken on the responsibility or guilt for her husband's anger.

What Can I Do About ~~Him?~~ Me?

Example 4: Spiritual Boundaries
Before Boundaries Were Set

Friend: *I have really been praying and thinking about what you should do. I know I have received an answer for you.*

Wife: *Well I am very interested in what you have received.*

Friend: *I think you should separate from your husband and teach him a lesson. He needs to get the message and so far he has not.*

Wife: *That's probably a good idea. I think I will do that.*

After Boundaries Were in Place

Friend: *I have really been praying and thinking about what you should do. I know I have received an answer for you.*

Wife: *Well, I'm interested to hear what you think, but I will make my decisions according to the spiritual direction I receive for myself.*

Friend: *I think you should separate from your husband and teach him a lesson. He needs to get the message and so far he has not.*

Wife: *Thanks for your opinion.*

When we have clear boundaries, we will not find it necessary to explain why we are doing something or why we are not doing something. We know inside why we have set the boundary, so we should not feel obligated to share all our reasoning with others. Because she had set her own spiritual boundaries, this wife was not unduly influenced by her friend's advice. She knew the source of her spiritual direction—and it was not her friend.

Example 5: Financial Boundaries
Before Boundaries Were Set

Wife: *I was just reviewing our bank statement and noticed that you cashed a $200 check that came out of our grocery money. What did you do with the money?*

Husband: *I had a slip-up and used the money for pornography.* (This assumes that her husband is actively repenting and is willing to tell the truth.)

Wife: *That's really hard on the family not to have the money for groceries like I had planned, but maybe I can find a way to get through until next pay day.*

Husband: *I'm sorry; I feel really bad.*

Wife: *It's okay; we'll get by somehow.*

After Boundaries Were in Place

Wife: *I was just reviewing our bank statement and noticed that you cashed a $200 check that came out of our grocery money. What did you do with the money?*

Husband: *I had a slip-up and used the money for pornography.* (This assumes that her husband is actively repenting and is willing to tell the truth.)

Wife: *That's really hard on the family not to have the money for groceries like I had planned. Using the family money for pornography is not acceptable. I need the $200 deposited back into the account. How will you do that?*

Husband: *I don't know because I don't get paid for another week or so.*

Wife: *I'm sorry about that, but I need the money in the account. We need groceries and I plan to go shopping on Thursday. Please make arrangements to get the money in the account.* (On his own, the husband may consider borrowing money from the bank, his parents, siblings, or a friend, but let him be responsible to replace the money.)

By having firm boundaries, the wife lets the natural consequences follow her husband's actions. She lets her husband find the solution to his own problem. She sets a deadline by planning to do her shopping on Thursday. The husband has a couple of days to resolve his problem and bear the consequences of his behavior. Even though it may be painful for the wife to see her husband lapse, she does not enable him by assuming any responsibility for his behavior.

Example 6: Sexual Boundaries
Before Boundaries Were Set

Husband: *I want you to…*

Wife: *Well, okay, I guess so.*

It appears that even though the wife felt uncomfortable with her husband's suggestion, she went along with it because she had not set any sexual boundaries. Afterwards, she likely felt that she had violated her own personal integrity because she had gone against her own feelings. This is an important area to consider—particularly when a husband has been addicted to pornography.

Sometimes, the wife hopes that going along with her husband's inappropriate requests may stop him from viewing pornography. The husband might even imply that it would. This is not true. Fulfilling lustful acts that a husband may have seen depicted in pornography, only reinforces, rewards, and enables his inappropriate cravings to continue. Instead of being supportive, the wife is enabling him to stay in lust, rather than cultivating the kind of loving, intimate relationship she really wants.

After Boundaries Were in Place

Husband: *I want you to . . .*

Wife: *I'm sorry, I am uncomfortable with that.*

It is more likely that we will set sexual boundaries if we clearly understand how damaging it is to the marriage for the husband to continue in lust. Only lust-free love and tenderness can truly enhance intimacy.

More On Setting Sexual Boundaries

A healthy, intimate, sexual relationship between husband and wife is one of God's greatest gifts to a married couple. It binds and unifies the couple as very few things can. However, if either spouse is using sex for validation, medication, or escape, it is not healthy. A healthy relationship combines an emotional connection with a sexual connection. Certainly, using sex as punishment is detrimental to individual healing and recovery within a marriage.

As was mentioned earlier, however, each partner should have and hold healthy and appropriate sexual boundaries for their own safety. Even though my husband and I have been seriously working on our own recovery for years, we are still refining our sexual relationship. In spite of past betrayals and pain, we now have a more intimate and fulfilling sexual relationship than we have ever had in our 40 years of marriage. I discovered as I have analyzed my past behavior, that I have been afraid to say what I need—and when I wasn't feeling safe. I did not always set boundaries well.

I know now, that my behavior was a desperate attempt to help myself feel better. Now we are both more comfortable in honestly expressing our feelings, which enhances the intimate nature of our sexual relationship. We have chosen to only engage sexually when we know that we are emotionally connected with each other. That boundary, for both of us, encourages us to stay connected on a daily basis.

Because sexual addicts have chosen sex as their drug of choice to medicate their stress or pain, boundaries need to be clear, and must be held to strongly from the beginning. Some therapists suggest a 90-day abstinence to start the rebuilding process, and I have seen that work very successfully. That abstinence gives both partners time to learn to connect emotionally and spiritually, without complicating things with sex. From the words of a professional, Dr. Mark Lasser, an internationally known speaker and author on the subject of sexual addiction,

> *Early on in recovery, sex addicts will need to observe a period of celibacy in order to reverse their belief that sex is their most important need. They also need to discover that sex is not the indicator of whether their spouse loves them, and their spouses need to learn that sex is not the way they please their partner. Abstinence takes the sexual pressure off the relationship so that the couple can work on play and communication during this time.*

Detachment and Boundary Setting

Even before setting boundaries, learning to detach appropriately is a concept critical to recovery. We should learn to detach ourselves from the agony of sexual addiction and obsession about the future. We should learn to detach from any desire to control or change other's emotions. We should allow others to feel their own emotions, but not let them control us. We can set boundaries, and decide that we will be happy and true to the person God wants us to become—regardless of the outcome. There will likely be pain, and probably a lot of "battle fatigue," but God will make everything right if we surrender to His will. The outcome is not up to us.

Such detachment is not detaching from the person we love; rather, it is detaching mentally and emotionally from the agony of involvement. We can't be happy in the present moment if we are involved emotionally in someone else's choices, particularly if their choices are destructive. There isn't a thing we can do about other people's choices, and the pain of worrying about them or trying to control them makes us feel crazy! It steals the joy that we could be experiencing right now. This is a true and life-changing concept. It is also a lot easier said than done.

Learning to detach takes a great deal of emotional energy and trust in God. It does *not* happen overnight. It takes constant effort and practice. It is a new way of thinking. When we are used to the validation or the connection we had, or thought we had, it's very difficult to detach emotionally and mentally. We become so vulnerable. It's not easy to share our true feelings, and risk losing relationships that we have been holding on to—even if they have been toxic or unhealthy.

In this context, the old saying comes to mind: "If you love someone, let them go. If they come back, they are yours. If they don't, they never were."

Another woman in our recovery group allowed me to share her experience. Her husband hasn't chosen recovery at this time, and has abandoned their family. She has no control over her husband's decisions, and has suffered intense pain and grief. She has had to detach emotionally in order to find peace and serenity as she moves forward with her life. She wrote of how she has had to detach:

> *Although I wasn't preventing my husband from seeing our children, I felt like my mother-in-law was rescuing and supporting him—setting up meetings for my husband to video chat with the girls online without me—making it easy for him to abandon us without consequences. I still love and respect my mother-in-law to this day, and I could sense her intense fear, so I wanted to make sure I was setting reasonable and rational boundaries with her.*
>
> *I called her after much prayer, and expressed my desire to have my husband be the one to take the initiative to see his daughters, and that he could contact me to make the arrangements. My mother-in-law lost it and spun into*

control mode—lecturing, blaming, shaming, and guilting me. She even yelled at me that it was my responsibility to make my husband see his children, even if he didn't want to. It was the first time I had felt blatantly disrespected by her. It was painful, but that experience only confirmed to me that I was making the correct decision to detach from her.

For the next several weeks, I worked intensely to stay healthy myself through the grief and trauma I experienced from losing the relationship I once had with her. She sent many more emails and texts that were manipulating and guilting. I worked very hard to not respond until I was in a good and healthy place, so that I wouldn't participate in the "drama" by giving in to her manipulation, or by saying things that I would regret, and so that I could stay true and connected to myself during this time.

With all the uncertainty in her life, this woman chose to detach from the agony of involvement. She continues to stay connected to God, herself, her family, and her support group. She is able to find peace, and even joy, as she takes one day at a time.

Boundaries Are for Safety—Not Punishment

Often, when we set healthy boundaries, our family, friends, or spouses cross the limits we have set. Boundaries, by our definition, must have consequences. Boundaries crossed without consequences are impotent. Though the temptation to do so can be overwhelming, we should not rescue people from the consequences of their choices.

We may have come to believe that rules or boundaries are for punishment. But they are not. The minute boundaries are about controlling someone else, they lose their potency.

Our teenage child may say, "I don't know why I have to be home at midnight. All my friends can stay out as late as they want! Don't you trust me?" We don't want to be the "mean mom" so we struggle, not knowing what we should do. But once we understand that boundaries are for safety, the right path becomes more clear. When we hold or enforce the boundary, we are really saying: "I love you and care about your safety and health, so you will need to be home by midnight or you can't go out tomorrow night."

When we don't enforce such a boundary, "Well okay—just this once," we are really saying: "I know that the best thing for you is to be home by midnight, but I don't care enough about you—or myself—to enforce that curfew. I care more about what you and your friends think of me."

Perhaps we believe that by allowing others to do whatever they want, without consequence, we are expressing our love. In reality, by not setting boundaries, we are expressing apathy. For example, God sets boundaries: they are called *commandments*. They are for our safety and well-being. He gives them to us for our protection because He loves us. They are not to punish us, but to invite us to come closer to *Him*. In that same manner, as we set boundaries we invite others close, and as a result foster more intimate relationships. It is a wonderful paradox!

One woman shared:

> *At first, setting boundaries felt like I was shoving everyone away, shutting out the world and callously shrugging off what I thought were commitments and responsibilities. In reality, it was the most vulnerable, loving thing I have ever done. I was saying for the first time in my life, "This is who I really am, and I am inviting you to be with me."*

Knowing Our Own Needs and Values

Too many women don't understand that we have the right and responsibility to protect ourselves from behavior that is inappropriate. Most often, failure or refusal to set boundaries comes from the fact that we simply aren't aware of what we want or need. We have lost ourselves. We may feel like we are being selfish if we are concerned about any of our own needs and wants. This is a completely wrong perception!

I have really tried to change the way I respond when asked about what I want. So I made a mental boundary. I tell myself, *Just make a choice—any choice.* I say, *This is what I want, and that's okay.* Deciding what I like has given me a zest for life and has enhanced my relationships.

For example, one day my granddaughter was coloring a picture for me and she asked, "What is your favorite color, Grandma?"

I thought, *I am working on my own recovery, and part of that is realizing that I have likes and opinions. I'm going to choose a favorite color right now and tell her.* I made a decision then and there, and said, "Bright pink."

Her eyes lit up, "I love that too!"

I hadn't thought of my favorite color for years! I felt an instant connection to myself, and just that much closer to my granddaughter.

The first step to creating and holding boundaries is recognizing who we are and what we need. Jennifer Schneider wrote, "Realistic boundaries cannot be established until one's self-esteem is high enough to place one's own needs above the need to please the spouse."[13] This following quote, also from Schneider, was critical in my understanding of my own recovery:

> Establishing boundaries *differs from* issuing ultimatums in an attempt to control the other person's behavior. Recovering coaddicts [afflicted spouses] determine which behaviors are unacceptable to them, and what they will do if those behaviors occur. Knowing the consequences, the addict can then choose what he/she wishes to do.[14]

I appreciate that Dr. Schneider reaffirms that the addict can choose to abide by the boundaries or not. We as wives cannot make that choice for them. To restate, using the example about my favorite color, if my granddaughter had grimaced and told me that bright pink was for old ladies, I would have laughed with her—and then still stuck with bright pink!

---

13 Jennifer P. Schneider, "Rebuilding the Marriage during Recovery from Compulsive Sexual Behavior," *Family Relations* 38, no. 3 (1989): 293.
14 Ibid.

One way for us to identify our needs is by writing a personal "Bill of Rights." It can reveal where your boundaries are, or areas in your life where you may need to set some.

I smiled when I read my friend's Bill of Rights. One read, "I have the right to have my hair the way I want, even if it's not in style." This is a physical boundary. Another read, "I have the right to be happy," an emotional boundary. And "I have the right to have a messy house," another physical boundary.

As I continued to read, I felt the deep soul-searching that had gone into her Bill of Rights. Her experience of coming to herself, and to God, has changed her life. Some of her other commitments read:

> *I have the right to expect my husband to honor his covenants and commitments to me.* [sexual/emotional boundary]
>
> *I have the right to walk away from, turn off, get rid of, or change any media that I feel is inappropriate in my home— or makes me afraid or uncomfortable—regardless of the situation that I am in and the way other people around me feel.* [spiritual/physical/social boundary]
>
> *I have the right to forgive my husband entirely.* [social/mental/spiritual boundary]

My friend had always retained these rights, but somewhere along the way she got confused and thought that it was better to always put other's opinions ahead of what was right for her. Writing her Bill of Rights dispelled the confusion.

Another right we have is to expect and request a thorough accounting of our husband's sexual behavior outside of our marriage. A full disclosure consisting of when such behaviors started, the frequency, types of behaviors and actions, and the last time there was any acting out, will be critical. This request often will be met with resistance, and a qualified sexual addiction therapist may be able to help here. We have found that without such total honesty, an addict cannot build a solid foundation from which to start recovery. A word of caution: as wives, we do not need to hear the gory details of exactly what he saw and did (body size, color of hair, etc.), because that may likely trigger our trauma, but we do need more information than men are usually willing to disclose at first.

There is also a serious health concern to take into account here. Many women have been exposed to sexually transmitted diseases without knowing it. Honest disclosure from a husband will help his wife determine how to protect and care for her health needs. I felt so much concern and sadness when one of my friends, a mother with young children, discovered a serious disease had been transmitted to her by her sex addict husband. So we need to be tested to take care of ourselves, and our husbands need to be very straightforward in helping us protect our health.

Along with understanding our own needs and rights, it is imperative that we have a strong sense of our own values. When a woman has been betrayed over and over by her husband, she may be tempted to take revenge. She may feel lonely and in need of validation, and it might seem only fair to find comfort in the arms of another man. This path will only lead to more trouble and deeper heartache than she already has. A few women I know have succumbed to this temptation, and then regretted it terribly afterward.

Other temptations that women may face is engaging in pornography and erotic materials on their own, or with their husband. Using these materials for escape, to dull the pain, or for "enhanced" intimate connection, will put us in as much danger of losing our soul to evil as it does men. It is crucial to set a boundary to keep promises to yourself and to God—regardless of what your husband's behavior might be. And to hold boundaries, we must maintain a strong sense of our own values, and listen to our own intuition or gut feeling.

I Happily Support Recovery Action and Behaviors

My personal motto is: *I will happily support recovery action and behaviors, but I refuse to enable addict behavior.* I set my boundaries around this statement.

Several years ago, when my husband and I had been working on recovery for a couple of years, I was feeling a disconnect from him, and my gut told me something was wrong. I felt like he was behind a brick wall and I couldn't get there, or even see him. I was reminded of the way things used to be, so I mentioned it to him.

I said, "It feels like you're distant. I don't know where you are, and I don't feel safe."

He said, "No, nothing's going on."

I had given myself permission to go with my gut, so a few minutes later I brought it up again. "I really feel like something is not quite right."

He was a little annoyed. "I can't think of anything," he responded. So I left it alone for some time. But then I remembered that I had committed months earlier to be true to myself and hold my personal emotional boundary. I told him that I was still feeling uncomfortable.

Finally, after a silence, he said, "There is something. I was triggered by a woman I saw on the street, and it bothered me. I thought I could just let it go."

For both my safety and his safety, we had set a boundary months before that if he told me within 24 hours that he had been triggered, then that was acceptable, but if he didn't, he would be sleeping a night in the other bedroom.

I said, "When was that?"

He said, "Well, it was on Monday."

"Today's Wednesday," I said.

There was silence. After a moment he said very quietly, "I guess I'll be sleeping in the other bedroom tonight."

Immediately my internal feelings shouted, *Oh no! That's too harsh. Now he's been honest and he's feeling remorseful, so the consequence shouldn't be necessary.* I wanted to soften the consequences for him.

But I stopped myself and just said, "Okay."

That night we prayed together, said good night, and then he went to sleep in the other bedroom. We didn't say much more about it.

As I lay in bed, the first feeling I felt was sadness. I really had wanted him to be with me. That feeling led me to feel that I had actually punished myself, and then I felt victimized and resentful. Next I felt anxious. We had been doing well for a long time, and I feared that holding this boundary would send him back into his addiction and make things bad again.

I could have let these feelings lead me into rescuing him from the consequence of his own choice, but I knew better. So I got re-centered, let go of these feelings, and trusted God. As I worked my own recovery in that moment, I felt a calming sense of peace and connection to myself and to God. I was really grateful for the skills I had learned that emphasized the importance of boundaries. I slept soundly. The next day there was a positive and connected feeling between us that was quite unexpected. We felt closer, and I felt safer in the relationship because I had been consistent *in my own recovery.*

Boundaries and Fear

Often, our own fears will keep us from holding boundaries. Once, at a recovery meeting, we were discussing how boundaries are necessary for safety. Afterward, a woman came up to me and said, "My husband has a stash of pornographic movies that he has been collecting since he was 17, and we have four children in our home."

I said, "Are you okay with that?"

She said, "No!"

I said, "Well, you might tell him that you need him to throw them out, and set an appropriate consequence. That would become your boundary for safety."

She said, "Oh, I wouldn't dare!"

Even though she was not comfortable with that kind of behavior, and the unsafe environment it posed for her own children, she was still too afraid of her husband's reaction to do anything about it. She was not being true to herself, and this inner conflict was creating anxiety and deep emotional exhaustion.

One woman called me recently and was so confused she could hardly put three coherent words together. She said, "I don't know why I'm calling you, but I've got to get some help." We spoke at length about boundaries.

Within four days she was able to say to her husband, "Your porn and masturbation in our home has got to stop. I need it to stop." In all her many years of marriage, she had never recognized that it was okay to stand up for herself and set appropriate boundaries. She also set a boundary that if he spoke unkindly to her or verbally abused her, she would leave the room.

We must stop being afraid of our addict husbands. We must look up to God with courage and faith. Our Heavenly Father does not condone the behaviors associated with sexual addiction, and He does not want His daughters to enable it. Do not be duped into calling it "forgiveness" and "unconditional love." God wants us to be faithful women of virtue. He wants our homes to be clean and free of this destructive material. He wants husbands and fathers to be faithful, kind, and loving. He will support and uphold us as we set appropriate boundaries.

Fear of the unknown often paralyzes us, and enables the addiction to continue. *I have come to the conclusion that if I base any decision on fear, it will always be the wrong decision.* Succumbing to fear is a relapse for me. To stay in recovery, I check in daily with myself and ask whether I have lived in fear, or if I have lived in the present moment, trusting God with the outcome.

Others' Reactions to Our Boundary Setting

Many women resolutely hold their boundaries in the face of threats, manipulation, criticism, or possibly violence—before things get better in their life. *Holding* boundaries is where the rubber meets the road in recovery.

It can be terrifying to set a boundary and hold it. In the beginning, we're not sure that we aren't just making things worse than they already are. One woman, recovering from her husband's multiple addictions said, "When we stop being a doormat, people *really* stomp their feet. Expect it to get worse before it gets better."

When we change the way we react or respond in a relationship, that change will likely upset the equilibrium in our families. Our loved ones are not used to the change and may be angry, defensive, or manipulative for a time. The atmosphere will improve as we hold our ground, with a belief that we truly are doing the most loving thing. But it will only get better when you get better.

A woman said:

> *I determined that I would have serenity, and I would have a good, healthy marriage—whether it was with my current husband or with someone else. And though I longed for my recovery to result in greater harmony with my spouse, in my particular case, it facilitated the (unexpectedly happy) ending of the relationship. I believe that my divorce was a natural result of my getting healthier and stronger emotionally.*
>
> *When you have a firm mission, when you stop bluffing and decide to choose serenity, working your program of recovery, those elements in your life that aren't contributing weed themselves out automatically—people either meet you, or they go away. By that time in my marriage, I was emotionally prepared for what happened.*

It might be necessary to start small and practice holding just one boundary. A sponsor who has worked her own recovery can be very helpful here. When you have given into threats and manipulation your whole life, it may be very difficult not to succumb to the temptation to return to your old ways. A friend of mine let me share her experience:

> *Looking back, I remember how scared I was to set the first tiny little boundary. I just wanted my husband to rearrange his study so he couldn't hide behind his computer and look at pornography. I had just opened up about my husband's addiction and started going to a 12 Step Group and therapy, so I had built some support.*
>
> *With the help of my sponsor, and a lot of prayer, I set a date for it to be done, and I told my husband, with tears in my eyes, that if it didn't happen by the set date, then I needed*

to call his parents, tell them about his addiction, and ask them for help. My husband agreed, but of course he didn't take me seriously, and when the date passed I knew I had to make a choice. It was difficult. I wished I hadn't even set a date. I thought, I will just give him a few more days. I'm sure he really wants to, but he's been busy.

Not this time. I knew that there was no going back. If I couldn't hold this boundary, things would never change. I had to call his parents. It was not a nice night. My husband threatened, swore, and yelled. Before he found out that I had already called his parents, he yanked the phone out of the wall, and when he found out, he drove off in his car. When he came back, he blamed me for ruining his relationship with his Dad forever, and spent the night in the basement. It was a scene out of a soap opera. It was terrible but I didn't back down. It's easy to see why I had never set a boundary before.

This was the beginning of a lot more boundaries which brought about necessary changes in our life. If I hadn't held that first boundary, I never would have changed. When I changed, he did too. *He thanks me now for what I did.*

Just like Bruiser the steer running wild, when we don't have boundaries, or when they are crossed with no consequences, there is no telling how much we will allow ourselves to be abused, or how we can ever find ourselves again. Let us round up our emotions, decide where we will draw the line, and ask for God's help to set firm boundaries with solid support in place.

Recently, one woman shared these feelings in our 12-Step meeting:

When we take care of our needs, listen to our intuition, and stay connected to ourselves, we are actually able to feel more connected to God. We are able to tap into an infinite source of validation and comfort. We no longer need our husbands to be our Higher Power, and we will be taught from heaven who we really are.

Do you love your family? If the answer is a resounding *Yes!* then you must set appropriate boundaries for the safety of your children, for yourself, *and* for your husband—especially if he is trapped in the life-crippling and spiritually damaging practice of pornography and sexual addiction. Trust that it is the most loving thing you can do. Supporting recovery behavior, and refusing to enable addict behavior, is about understanding who we are—what we want and what we need—being true and honest to ourselves, and sticking to what we believe.

What I Can Do

FORGIVENESS IS NOT THE SAME AS *TRUST*

Shortly after we had moved to a new home, a grey striped cat adopted our family. He climbed up on our porch and begged for food. Out of pity we fed him one meal, and from thenceforth he was a member of our family. Since he slept on the mat outside, we called him Mat the Cat.

Mat was really good natured with children. Occasionally, the kids would bring him in the house and he'd snuggle up to our little boys. However, if one of the older boys or my husband walked close to him, he'd scramble. He would run just far enough to be out of their reach, then turn and stare suspiciously at whatever man had just walked by. He was especially fearful if one of the men got close to him with their feet. After we observed this behavior several times, we figured that at some point in Mat's life an adult man had probably kicked him badly. Although no one in our family would ever hurt him, he continued to fearfully distance himself to protect himself.

As my husband and I spent hours talking and trying to work through the difficulties of his betrayal and my fear, I came to appreciate that look in Mat's eyes. I had been kicked so many times that I too had a difficult time trusting. Even though my husband was making major efforts to change, I still felt a need to protect myself from possible further damage.

So protection and safety were among my first goals. I didn't want to live my life in a constant state of fear, but I also didn't want to be "kicked" again. I needed to keep myself safe—physically and emotionally. As for Mat the Cat, he began to recognize that the men in our family would not be mean to him—but he still kept his distance. He did become more trusting, but it took a lot of time. I recognized that same process working in me as well. Trust once broken is hard to regain. It takes time to earn back. This is a slow process.

Over the many years of my experience with my husband's addiction, I truly wanted to forgive and trust him, but I have learned that *forgiveness* and *trust* are not the same. After 32 years of his sexual betrayals, I could no longer trust him. Throughout my recovery, I have learned some valuable lessons that have helped my husband and me rebuild trust and obtain forgiveness in our relationship. Both are possible to achieve given hard work and sufficient time.

A Caution

Here I must pause and offer words of caution. If you or your children are in danger in any way, please separate yourself and them from the abusing person, find legal help, and obtain social support as soon as possible. There are many forms of abuse: verbal, physical, sexual, and emotional. If such abuse is taking place, please seek help immediately. Trusting someone who is a danger to you or your children is unwise. We don't want to be foolish in our willingness to trust when that person has not shown us trustworthy behavior. Our own safety, and the safety of our family, should come before trust. I urge you to determine your level of personal safety and the safety of your children, and if necessary, take appropriate action immediately.

Rebuilding Trust

One evening, my husband and I gave a presentation to a large group of adults. After the meeting, a few people came up to ask us questions and express appreciation. I noticed one man who stood back patiently and waited until everyone else had gone. He finally approached me and boldly asked, "Do you *totally* trust your husband?" I was taken aback. I realized that he wanted total honesty from me. It would have been easy to say, "Yes, I totally trust him!" but that would not have been truthful. So I answered, "Not totally. He is working on earning my trust, and I am working on learning to trust him."

So how do we begin this process? First, let us recognize that building trust in a relationship takes time. It takes a lot of time, especially when there have been long-term betrayals. In order to feel safe in my own marriage, I look for actions in my husband about which I can say, "Now that's trustworthy behavior." For example, he calls me when he says he is going to call, he comes home when he says he will, he goes to his 12-Step recovery meetings, and he goes to church on time, and fulfills his responsibilities there. Each of these actions, combined with a humble attitude, show me that he is trustworthy in many different areas of life—not just in our relationship. As I notice those trustworthy actions, I give him credit for what he is doing, and I allow my general trust in him to grow little by little.

In an effort to re-build trust in our marriage, we focus on *recovery*—not *sobriety*. Because my husband can be sober but not in recovery, I try to be aware of addict behaviors such as lying, minimization, justification, blaming, emotional distance, or denial. If my husband is exhibiting such addict behaviors, trust cannot grow. On the other hand, when I see recovery behaviors such as kindness, patience, selflessness, humility, empathy, and love, I know that I am safe to begin trusting him more.

Also, my husband and I have a habit of checking in with each other every night, which further builds trust. We use what Dr. Brené Brown calls the *Vowel Check-In*.[15]

At the end of each day, my husband and I come together and tell each other about different aspects of our day, based on the vowels, *A E I O U Y*.

A is for *abstinent*. We each ask of ourselves, "Have I been abstinent today?" We know what abstinence means for each of us. For him, did he

---

15 Brené Brown, *The Gifts of Imperfection: Let Go of Who You Think You're Supposed to Be and Embrace Who You Are* (Center City, MN: Hazelden Publishing, 2010), 74.

lust, experience triggers, or act out in any way? For me, did I go to a place of fear, judgment, or control during that day?

E is for *exercise*. Did I take time to do some physical exercise?

For *I*, we ask "Did *I* do something for myself today?"

O is "Did I do something for *others*?"

U is "Are there any *unexpressed* emotions that I need to share?"

Y is "What is the '*yay!*' for today?" meaning the happy and exciting things that happened during the day.

We have found that using this simple acronym has become a great check-in tool, and helps us build trust in our marriage!

After hearing about this process you may ask yourself, *What if he doesn't want to check in?* Of course, that's his choice. But you still check in, and account for yourself. Always remember that this is about *your* recovery. After checking in, you might say, "It would mean a lot to me for you to check in, too." If we consistently check in, we not only give ourselves time to share how our day is going with our spouse, but we provide for them an opportunity to regularly check in with us as well.

Along with using the Vowel Check-In, we have also begun to include a dialogue concerning my trauma. I have learned that it is natural for spouses of addicts to occasionally re-experience trauma—even after long periods of recovery. Even though we have worked through a lot of our issues over the last seven years of our recovery, the pain may occasionally resurface. The more my husband works his own recovery, the more he comes to accept that he created and caused much of my pain. His recognition of this is a vital element to our healing. We want to build a thriving relationship in which he understands—without any defensiveness or blaming—that I have been traumatized, and that I won't "just get over it." So in our efforts to create a thriving relationship, we have come upon a simple dialogue, one we call "the script."[16] It starts by him saying,

> *The fact that you… [are reacting and feeling this way right now], is evidence that… [you have been hurt by my behavior in the past].*

---

16 Todd Olson, a therapist at the Lifestar Network, developed this technique.

No wife should...[ever have to go through that kind of pain], and for that I am very sorry.

I want to reassure you that...[I am working on my recovery]. Again, I am sorry.

What can I do for you right now?

That script, that short dialogue, when said in a humble way, melts my heart. When he is in a place of humility, I feel that he understands my pain and wants to think about my needs, which fosters in me a desire to trust him.

These are some of the ways that we choose to build trust in our relationship. Remember that in your journey, rebuilding trust takes place one day at a time, and is always specific to your own needs. My husband and I have built a stronger, safer relationship, but it has not been instantaneous and it has not been easy.

Forgiveness Is a Gift

When the man at the presentation asked me if I trusted my husband, I responded, "Not totally." But if he would have asked me if I had *forgiven* my husband, I would have said, "Yes." It has been a long process though, because ironically, forgiveness is a gift that I give to *my* soul. The ability to forgive comes from God, and I can choose to accept its healing power. Without it, I have no peace.

The crucial difference between forgiveness and trust is this: trust is earned; forgiveness is given freely. And when trust is broken, it must be earned again—one experience, one day at a time. Forgiveness, on the other hand, is not conditioned upon apologies or restitutions on the part of the offender. It is "a response to being wronged that entails a change of heart in which justified anger, resentment, or indignation is given up" by the person who has been hurt.[17] Likewise, "forgiveness annuls not the wrong

---

17 Frank Fincham, "Forgiveness: Does It Matter?" (lecture, Brigham Young University, Provo, UT, November 29, 2011).

itself, but the distorting effect that this wrong has upon one's relations with the wrongdoer."[18]

Forgiveness does not mean condoning offensive behavior. Dr. Jennifer Schneider, a nationally recognized physician specializing in sexual addictions, said:

> *Forgiving is not the same as tolerating. If the addict does not perceive a problem and is unwilling to change his/her behavior, the spouse may decide to leave. If the addict does want to save the marriage, forgiving [the addict] will be easier if the addict not only acknowledges the pain caused, but also shows evidence of commitment to change.*[19]

Forgiving is not synonymous with forgetting. "It is not possible to remove the offence from the consciousness."[20] This means it is not possible to completely forget the hurtful actions of our loved ones. We can use these memories as the basis of knowledge for our future safety; yet we should not dwell on those actions in unnecessary or destructive ways.

Forgiveness is a process and cannot be rushed by us or our offending spouse. In that process, we should share our honest emotions as we feel them. Researchers suggest that "although negative behaviors [our expressions of anger and grief] may indeed be unsatisfying initially, they *can* motivate necessary changes in the partner."[21] Such negative statements predicted positive change in the partner one year later.[22] In other words, when one spouse expresses his or her honest emotions concerning the offensive behavior of the other, those emotions may actually be a catalyst for improved behavior and relationship change in a year's time. Consider also that forgiving too quickly, or too easily, may create harm and encourage

---

18 Ibid.
19 Frank Fincham, "Forgiveness: Does It Matter?" (lecture, Brigham Young University, Provo, UT, November 29, 2011).
20 Frank D. Fincham, Julie Hall, and Steven R. H. Beach, "Forgiveness in Marriage: Current Status and Future Directions," *Family Relations, 55* (October 2006): 415-27, 416.
21 James K. McNulty, "The Dark Side of Forgiveness: The Tendency to Forgive Predicts Continued Psychological and Physical Aggression in Marriage," *Personality and Social Psychology Bulletin* 37 (2011): 770-83, http://psp.sagepub.com/content/37/6/770, 779.
22 Ibid.

the offender to continue transgressions.²³ Therefore, when there have been serious, ongoing transgressions, forgiveness may often and necessarily be a slow process.

Forgiveness often occurs over a series of steps. Dr. Schneider gives a few markers for what needs to occur in this process:

> • *The first step of forgiveness for the betrayed spouse is to recognize that a wrong has been done to him/her. Many insecure spouses have excuses and explanations for their partner's actions; instead, they must accept that a real wrong was done to them.*
>
> • *Next they need to feel the pain, anger, and possibly hate which the addict's actions caused. This may be new to them if they are used to suppressing and hiding feelings.*
>
> • *Then comes sharing the strong feelings with others— ideally, by confronting the addict, otherwise by expressing feelings to their counselor or support group.*
>
> • *The next step is to see the addict not as a romantic figure who can fulfill all the spouse's needs, but rather as the imperfect compulsive person that he/she is.*²⁴

I took time to express to my husband my sadness and even anger at what had happened in my life. It was part of my process of forgiving him.

Many of us fear that by forgiving, we give up power, and may be viewed by outsiders as weak or unwise. Remember that forgiving others is a gift you give *yourself* to find peace of mind. Gandhi said, "The weak can never forgive. Forgiveness is the attribute of the strong."²⁵ I want to be one of the strong.

---

23 Ibid.
24 Schneider, "Rebuilding the Marriage during Recovery," 291.
25 Mahatma Gandhi, *The Collected Works of Mahatma Gandhi*, vol. 51, *January 6, 1931-April 28, 1931* (New Delhi: Publications Division Government of India, 1999), http://www.gandhiserve.org/cwmg/cwmg.html, 302.

What Can I Do About ~~Him?~~ Me?

Trusting God and Myself

After so many betrayals, I was fearful that I would never know if my husband was being truthful, or if I could trust him. But with the knowledge and education I gained through therapy, the 12-Step program, and other resources, I now have the tools and the confidence to know what recovery action and behavior look like. In addition to these tools, I am willing to trust my instincts; I trust that God will let me know if I am safe or not.

When my husband and I share our story, I suspect that many people may think, *"Does the elevator not go to the top with that woman? Is she totally clueless? Because nobody should stay that long."* My response is that since I was 18, my guiding scripture has been, "Trust in the Lord with all thine heart and lean not unto thine own understanding. In all thy ways acknowledge Him, and He shall direct thy paths."[26] People hear my story and frequently ask me, "Why did you stay?" I stayed because when I kept asking God, "Should I stay or should I leave?" God kept answering, "Hang in there with me. Stay for now." It is because I trusted in the Lord and His inspiration that I am here today.

Because all humans have sins and we all make mistakes, we must trust in God first. When I do that, He takes care of me. That does not mean that we will not have trials or temptations. It does mean that when we place our trust in Him first, we cannot be devastated by someone else's behavior. Only when I lose trust and faith in the Lord, do I begin to fear that someone else's actions might destroy me. Trusting in God is where I keep my focus—one day at a time.

Years ago, I could have never imagined that I would still be married to my husband today. Forgiveness and trust seemed an impossibility, but now I am grateful to acknowledge they have become a reality for us—with the help of the Lord.

---

26 Proverbs 3:5.

What I Can Do

I CAN'T BUT *HE* CAN, AND I WILL LET *HIM*

I was 56 years old and inching my way toward a degree in marriage and family studies at Brigham Young University. My peers were not only very bright and talented students, but also between the ages of 19 and 23. I was just plain afraid most days. I wondered, *What will happen if I fail this test? What will my professor think of me if I do poorly on this assignment? How do I use Google docs? How can I ever understand physics now without having studied it first as a young person?* My fears ran rampant.

I learned a valuable lesson concerning my fear as a student at BYU. One day in my biology class, there was a little mouse in a cage at the front of the room. As I left class, the professor stopped me: "Rhyll, come here." I don't know why he singled me out, except perhaps because I was the only grandma-old lady there!

I walked over to the professor and noticed the mouse staring up at me with its beady eyes.

"I want you to hold this mouse," the professor said.

"Oh no, I can't! I *hate* mice!" I exclaimed, looking for a chair to stand on and scream. (It's the safest thing to do with a mouse in the room. Trust me.) I really, really hate mice. Give me snakes and spiders any day, but mice? No, thank you. I have had a fear of rats and mice since I was six years old. As a little girl growing up in the mountains of Montana, I would occasionally spot one of the monstrous pack rats that took up residence in the shed behind our home. They were very frightening to me. Fifty years later, that fear remained just as intense as ever.

"No, I want you to hold it," my professor said firmly.

I thought for a moment. I could either walk away, refusing to even try, or I could surrender my fear and hold that tiny mouse.

I closed my eyes and held out my cupped hands.

My professor brought the tiny mouse out of the cage and gave it to me. I was so afraid. I could feel that little mouse's body in my hands, and I also could feel its warmth and the softness of its fur. And then…I surrendered my fear. It was almost as if a voice said to me, "Let go of the fear." The change was a physical one for me. I literally felt the fear and anxiety leave my body. I stood there, silently holding the mouse in my hands, and opened my eyes. The professor then took the mouse back, put it in the cage, smiled, and said nothing. I wanted to cry, but held my emotions in check as I walked out of the room.

That brief experience had a profound impact on me. Although a small thing, I nearly let fear keep me from holding that mouse. But when I surrendered my fear and held out my hands, I realized that I just didn't have to be afraid. I couldn't control that mouse—the long-held representation of my fear—so I had to trust in God that I would be all right. And I was.

Fear

In the beginning of my journey toward recovery, I did not know much about the 12-Step program. When I finally started attending, the first few meetings were very uncomfortable for me. I left these feeling confused and fearful. The language they used was foreign to me, and I regularly felt fear, sadness, and hopeless.

I was clearly in a state of denial. After all, *my* husband had come out with his third disclosure and had been arrested for prostitution. Even though three years had passed since his arrest, I was still afraid of divorce and all the bitterness it would likely create for our children. And I still worried that I might be homeless and unable to financially care for myself.

During those three years, my husband had changed through his valiant efforts in recovery, but that didn't change me. *I* was still afraid, and *my* life was still out of control. Although I didn't always see it, I too needed a 12-Step program—designed specifically for my own unique needs and healing.

Attending a 12-Step meeting for families of sex addicts for the first time is a difficult experience for most afflicted spouses. When I meet with a newcomer to the program, I share how I was once resistant, and stress the importance of giving it a try. I always encourage women to come at least six times before they make a decision about whether or not it is for them.

One woman spoke with me about her first few experiences with the meetings. Though she felt uncomfortable in the same ways I did at first, she stuck with it, because she also felt safe. She said:

> *My first meeting was strange, and I cried the whole way through it. I felt really stupid and mad. I was not going to go again. At the end, the other women challenged me to come for at least six times before giving up. It took two weeks of not going before I decided to try again. I think I only went again because I wanted my husband to go [to his meetings], so I went too.*
>
> *At first, the strongest impression I had was that I was in a room with very strong and beautiful women. I could feel their strength and I wanted it. They scared me, and sometimes I hated them. But I saw and felt something that I knew I wanted and needed. I also remember the safety that I felt. The platform for sharing—with no cross talk and no gossip—made me feel safe enough to share.*

Like me, this woman was met with a new vocabulary that might be intimidating for some at first. Nevertheless, she stayed, was determined to learn, and as a result found a source of hope. Beginning, and then continuing to attend a 12-Step group, is crucial for obtaining the hope and support that leads to the recovery, which we are all seeking. We can find the words, the education, and the hope we need in this setting.

Frustration

As well as feeling fearful, I often felt frustrated. I couldn't understand why I needed to go to meetings when this was clearly my husband's problem. My *husband's* life was unmanageable, I thought, but *I* was doing just fine, thank you very much.

We may often feel we're attending only because of somebody else's behavior. That's typical for most of us at the beginning. After all, somebody else's behavior in fact did bring us to this point. So if he would just fix his behavior, or if we could help fix him, then, we argue, we won't have any problems ourselves. This is part of the reason why we don't face our own recovery—we feel that we simply don't have anything to recover from.

It takes attending probably six to eight meetings before we may realize that the reason we're there is not because of somebody else's behavior; rather, we come because it is a spot of safety. I remember the first time I recognized that surrender, and it was a great blessing to me. A woman at the 12-Step program had shared with me the deepest pain and desire of her heart, and I started to feel connected to myself in such an honest and raw way—something I had never felt in any other setting. In these meetings we are understood and we can learn how to deal with our challenges from our own perspective.

In my case, I discovered that even if my husband didn't have a sexual addiction, I would still need to figure out who I am. That's what 12-Step meetings have done for me. The longer I go, the more I understand how much I need them. Going over and over the 12 Steps is critical for me, as is actually working them, consulting with my sponsor, and being accountable for my own behavior. I have had to accept that trauma doesn't automatically go away in six months, a year, or even two. It is a process, and the bitter feelings of anger, fear, and frustration do come back occasionally—even when my husband is in recovery. That's when I need help, I need support, and I need education.

It took attending multiple meetings, and careful personal study of the 12 Steps, for me to realize just how out of control my life was. And once I realized this, the 12-Step program started to really work for me. It wasn't that the group was different—I was different.

Fortification

12-Step programs share a number of common elements that aid in the recovery and surrendering process. Let's briefly look at each one.

Openness

Meetings provide a safe, supportive environment to share feelings and experiences with others who understand what you are going through ,because they have experienced the same thing.

Specific Boundaries and Recovery Plan

A 12-Step program can provide specific rules and definitions of abstinence or sobriety that are used to measure progress and recovery. The program also offers literature and instructions for recovery that can be used daily to help individuals.

Accountability

Afflicted spouses check in frequently with a sponsor, and also report their progress at meetings. These interactions provide accountability and transparency. They also help to dissipate the shame surrounding addiction, so the spouse can focus on the actions needed to achieve recovery.

Support

Recovering addicts share their experience, strength, and hope with new members who are just starting the recovery process.

Newer, as well as more experienced afflicted spouses in recovery, all find support and encouragement by attending meetings, talking with other group members, making outreach calls, reading literature, working with a sponsor, or serving as a sponsor.

Focus on a Higher Power

All 12-Step programs focus on turning to a Higher Power for intervention and healing.[27] I believe that this is the most important factor in achieving recovery. In fact, if you get to the end of this book and haven't recognized the importance of involving God in your recovery, the central goal of this book will not have been achieved.

Surrendering Through the 12 Steps

The first three steps of the program are all about accepting, believing in, and surrendering to God. They are defined in this way:

> **Step 1.** *My life is unmanageable, and I can't control everything around me; but*

> **Step 2.** *I believe in God, and that through His power He can bring me peace and serenity in my life; and*

> **Step 3.** *Through my agency and my choices, I will let Him.*

The first step implies realizing that there are many things in my life that I cannot control. On paper my life looked pretty good: big house, seven kids, and cute, thrifty outfits. But because I was attempting to control every part of my life, admitting that circumstances in my life were out of control was very scary. I had never seen my life as unmanageable, but "unmanageability" means that there were things I thought I could control but in fact I could not. I even compared myself to others whose lives appeared more dysfunctional on the outside than mine. I thought, *Those people's lives are really unmanageable, and relatively speaking, mine is going just fine.* This comparison—and fear—lead me to deny the true unmanageability of my life. You see, fear had governed many aspects of my life; it had paralyzed me from doing things that I needed to do and from

---

27   S. A. Lifeline Foundation, *Understanding Pornography and Sexual Addiction*, 22.

being who I wanted to be. But at that defining moment on the lawn after my husband's third disclosure, I knew without a shadow of a doubt that my life was truly unmanageable. I also knew that that unmanageability extended into every part of my life, including my family, my marriage, my finances, and my future.

The second step of the 12 Steps is realizing that there is a great, all-knowing God who can care for me in my life. He can lead me and guide me. After standing on the lawn and relinquishing my control, I walked into the house and spoke to my sons. I bore testimony of my belief in God and His care for me. I told them, "I don't know what's going to happen, but I know that God will take care of us."

The third step of the 12 Steps is deciding that through my agency and choices, I will let God guide me to serenity. I will let go of my self-will. This happens to be one of the hardest things I am doing. I am reminded daily that I must let go and "let God"—the only power that can truly lead me to peace.

These first three steps are often a daily process of learning to surrender my will to God through believing in His great power. For most of us, surrendering our will to God is one of the most difficult things we may ever do. One spiritual leader has said:

> *The submission of one's will is really the only uniquely personal thing we have to place on God's altar. The many other things we "give," ..., are actually the things He has already given or loaned to us. However, when you and I finally submit ourselves, by letting our individual wills be swallowed up in God's will, then we are really giving something to Him! It is the only possession which is truly ours to give!*[28]

I have discovered that surrendering is an emotional, physical, and spiritual process directing me to God. I can't merely *say* that I will surrender my fear: I have to work through these steps daily. They guide

---

28 Neal A. Maxwell, "'Swallowed Up in the Will of the Father,'" *Ensign*, November 1995, http://www.lds.org/ensign/1995/11/swallowed-up-in-the-will-of-the-father.

me one day at a time through all the problems I face—whether big or small—in all areas of my life. That is surrendering my fears to God.

On My Knees, on the Phone, in the Box

If the surrender process isn't firmly in place, it's rather easy for me to go to a place of fear. When I'm at the mall with my husband and I'm afraid something is triggering him, it's easy to go to a place of fear. When certain commercials come on TV while we're relaxing together, it's easy to go to a place of fear. Fear is easy. To deal with those feelings of fear and maintain peace in my life, the surrender process is essential. For me, the process of surrendering has three parts: on my knees, on the phone, in the box.

On my knees consists of giving my fear to Heavenly Father through spiritual conversation. I say to Him in prayer, "I feel so much pain. I can't control it. Please take it from me."

On the phone requires that I call someone who understands my fear. This is typically a sponsor who is also working through the program and appreciates what I'm going through because she has gone through it too. I can tell my sponsor that something has happened and I am afraid, or I feel angry or unsafe. This person will understand my concerns, and encourage me to work through the process of surrender.

One woman told me of her struggles with opening up to a sponsor. She said:

> *I wanted my marriage and my life to be completely different. It was said in a meeting that we should be calling a sponsor every day. I thought that was crazy. I thought to myself,* Talk about codependence! *However, I started to call my sponsor. It was very hard. It was the hardest part of the whole process. I can see now why it was so hard: because no one had ever helped me before when I had asked for help. It wasn't that they didn't want to; it's that they didn't understand. They had absolutely no idea how to deal with sexual addiction and codependence. I would dial my sponsor with my fingers literally trembling.*

> *I was so shy, ashamed, scared, prideful, and codependent! I thought I needed to rescue my sponsor from myself. I was mad at her.*
>
> *For the first month, it seemed like all she said was work on steps one, two, and three, and live in the present moment. She took the emphasis off my husband and put it on me! I can't tell you why I kept going, except that I wanted recovery; and now I knew a few people on the planet who had it, and I was going to keep bugging them until I got it.*

In the box means to write this phrase on a little piece of scrap paper: "I surrender to my Heavenly Father…[my fear]." I put this piece of paper in what I call my Surrender Box. (Some women call it their God Jar.) Then I walk away from it. I remind myself that I cannot change anybody else, and that I want peace to dwell inside me, without fear or control.

Every time a thought, feeling, or situation comes that pushes me out of a peaceful serene place, I do these three actions, and then I choose to let it go. Sometimes it requires doing this multiple times a day if I am really obsessing about something. For some reason, it requires these physical, emotional, and spiritual actions in order to bring my "crazy-committee" back to order. I cannot control my husband's behavior, my son's behavior, or anyone else's behavior for that matter! I can only cultivate the peaceful feeling that I desire to have inside of me. Peace is the sweetest blessing of surrender.

One woman shared with me her powerful story of surrender:

> *I was married to my husband for twelve years, and didn't learn until after I left him, that he'd had an addiction to pornography. By the time I left him he was spending up to sixteen hours a day online, and he was getting in trouble with his boss for not completing his paperwork.*
>
> *Over the years, our marriage had become a living hell as he grew increasingly emotionally, verbally, and physically abusive.*

What Can I Do About ~~Him?~~ Me?

Six months after we separated, my daughters, ages five and eight, began disclosing sexual abuse at the hands of their father, which by all accounts had been happening all their lives. Because I hadn't caught him "in the act," and disclosures made by children are not considered proof, my daughters began having to spend time with their father, despite their healthy instincts to separate themselves from him. It was heartbreaking to watch "the system" force them to have a relationship with the man who had hurt and terrorized them so badly.

Eventually, the time came when my daughters would soon have to spend the night unsupervised in his home. As the day approached, I fell apart. I fasted and prayed, but experienced a fear so debilitating I could no longer feel any connection with God, the universe, or anyone or anything. Looking back, I can see that my fear was multiplying so quickly, and I was holding onto it so tightly that I couldn't feel God's presence in my life, nor could I feel Him working to free me.

Luckily, I had recently joined a 12-Step group, and I learned from my sponsor a process of surrendering my fears—on my knees, on the phone, in the box. I didn't see how a process so simple could help me, but I agreed to give it a try. As I surrendered my biggest fear, the safety of my daughters, I pictured angels coming to carry my fear to God, and I pictured me placing my daughters into Christ's arms for safekeeping.

Within about half an hour, I was amazed to realize my fear had left me. One by one, I surrendered my fears every time they surfaced. Within a day or two, this process had uncovered my real emotions, which before had been completely obscured by the fear. And while my daughters were with their father, I was able to experience empowerment and even joy.

This process seemed almost magical, and I feel so blessed to have found it.

Having done everything that she possibly could, this woman was able to find peace of mind from the anguish and despair through the surrender process—which is really a process of turning our hearts, our minds, and our will over to God. Surrender means admitting that we are powerless, which in turn means that the outcomes of everything—including our marriages—are not completely in our hands.

I love the lyrics to this hymn. They have often blessed me and given me strength in times of need.

Fear not, I am with thee; oh, be not dismayed,
For I am thy God and will still give thee aid.
I'll strengthen thee, help thee, and cause thee to stand...
Upheld by my righteous, omnipotent hand.

When through the deep waters I call thee to go,
The rivers of sorrow shall not thee o'erflow,
For I will be with thee, thy troubles to bless...
And sanctify to thee thy deepest distress.

When through fiery trials thy pathway shall lie,
My grace, all sufficient, shall be thy supply.
The flame shall not hurt thee; I only design...
Thy dross to consume, and thy gold to refine.[29]

---

29 [Robert Keen], "How Firm A Foundation," in *Hymns of The Church of Jesus Christ of Latter-day Saints* (Salt Lake City: The Church of Jesus Christ of Latter-day Saints, 2002), 85.

What I Can Do

GRATITUDE IN THE PRESENT MOMENT

One afternoon as I looked around the dinner table where all my children sat talking, laughing, and enjoying dinner together, I felt intense gratitude and joy for the blessing of being with my family. I sat back and tried to take it all in and bask in those wonderful feelings. In that moment, I did not know that my husband was hiding such awful secrets, that he was living a double life, and that I was being betrayed. But did that diminish my feelings of joy? No. I truly felt blessed at that time, and knowing my husband's secrets *now* does not make those feelings *then* a lie in my life. Someone else's behavior does not need to determine my happiness—past or present.

Count Your Many Blessings

After my husband's second disclosure of his behavior, I felt shattered. Ten years previously, he had promised me he was never going to sexually act out again. So I felt betrayed because he had lied to me for so many years. A thousand questions were racing through my mind: How much of our life together has been a lie? How many times had he been involved in sacred experiences with our family and served unworthily in church callings? It was very hard for me to reconcile this level of deception.

What Can I Do About ~~Him?~~ *Me?*

I went to my ecclesiastical leader and asked if he would pray with me. The entire message of his prayer was, "Count your blessings." I was surprised to say the least, because I wanted some answers to my questions: What should I do? Should I stay in the marriage? How can I keep myself safe? What am I going to do with my children to protect us from further betrayal? Yet instead of direct answers to my questions, the whole prayer directed me to "count your blessings."

A couple of weeks later I went to a sacred place of worship. I went petitioning God for help and answers. Nothing came. I prayed for a long time, pleading for some guidance, but no answer came. As I walked away, questioning whether God was even hearing my prayers, these words from the hymn "Count Your Blessings" came to my mind: "When upon life's billows you are tempest-tossed, When you are discouraged, thinking all is lost, Count your many blessings; name them one by one, And it will surprise you what the Lord has done."[30]

I thought, "Really? I am completely devastated, and this is the answer I'm getting?"

Probably a week later, I was still seeking an answer. I read in my scriptures the direction to be "giving thanks always for all things unto God and the Father in the name of our Lord Jesus Christ."[31] I thought, "Okay! I get it! I don't know how this is my answer, but obviously it is. I will strive to be grateful." As I look back now, it was the answer. God wanted me to look for the positive in my life. He also wanted me to see His hand in my life. He knew that if I did, it would help sustain me and give me peace. Gratitude to Him would help me to find my own recovery.

Gratitude in Suffering

One of my favorite books is *The Hiding Place*. The story of the Ten Boom sisters and their experience in a Nazi prison camp is moving and inspirational to me. Corrie and Betsie Ten Boom were horrified by the

---

30 Johnson Oatman Jr., "Count Your Blessings," in *Hymns of The Church of Jesus Christ of Latter-day Saints* (Salt Lake City: The Church of Jesus Christ of Latter-day Saints, 2002), 241.
31 Ephesians 5:20.

miserable and devastating circumstances in the camp, and soon discovered that the barracks to which they had been assigned were full of fleas. Corrie wondered how they could survive in such a place. It was Betsie who discovered God's answer in her scriptures:

> *"'Rejoice always, pray constantly, give thanks in all circumstances; for this is the will of God in Christ Jesus.'"*
>
> *"That's it, Corrie! That's His answer. 'Give thanks in all circumstances!' That's what we can do. We can start right now to thank God for every single thing about this new barracks!*[32]*"*

So they thanked God for the fact they were together. They thanked God they had a Bible. They even thanked God for the horrible crowds of prisoners, that more people would be able to hear God's word. And then, Betsie thanked God for the fleas:

> *The fleas! This was too much. "Betsie, there's no way even God can make me grateful for a flea."*
>
> *"'Give thanks in all circumstances,'" she quoted. "It doesn't say, 'in pleasant circumstances.' Fleas are part of this place where God has put us.'*
>
> *And so we stood between piers of bunks and gave thanks for fleas. But this time I was sure Betsie was wrong.*[33]

But she was not wrong. The fleas had kept the guards out of their barracks and protected these women from abuse, harassment, and worse things. The fleas were actually a gift from God.

I too could not see in the midst of my despair that there were blessings from God coming to me. After all these years, I now look back and recognize

---

32 Corrie ten Boom, *The Hiding Place*, with John and Elizabeth Sherrill (Grand Rapids: Chosen Books, 1996), 180.
33 Ibid., 181.

how much growth and refinement my experiences have given me. As the author Victor Frankl said, "Suffering ceases to be suffering at the moment it finds a meaning."[34]

Gaining Perspective

In the midst of affliction, we often cannot see the big picture; we cannot see the meaning. All we can do, it seems, is live in the present moment, find the small and simple ways God presents His hand in our lives, and trust that there is a purpose.

There have been times when I've been on my knees experiencing a great deal of grief, when suddenly, I've felt His love. It doesn't come in that way all the time, but I have repeatedly received such a comfort that I know comes directly from heaven. Some days that doesn't come, often because I'm not open to receive that feeling. But I still continue to look for ways that He shows me His love.

I'm aware that some individuals believe God's love is very distant, that it's not personal. They may believe that God is a judgmental God, and that He's all about justice, or that God loves everybody all the same and that it's not something you can personally feel. But I believe He knows and loves each one of us personally.

It has been found through research, that gratitude actually changes people's lives. Those who count their blessings or find things to be grateful for each day have fewer health complaints, feel happier about their lives, and have more positive affects in their relationships than those who don't.[35] Such a marked difference, and all from counting blessings!

---

34 Viktor E. Frankl, *Man's Search for Meaning* (New York: Washington Square Press, 1985), 135.
35 Robert A. Emmons and Michael E. McCullough, "Counting Blessings Versus Burdens: An Experimental Investigation of Gratitude and Subjective Well-Being in Daily Life," *Journal of Personality and Social Psychology* 84, no. 2 (2003): 377–89, doi:10.1037/0022-3514.84.2.377.

Building an Attitude of Gratitude

Let me encourage you to begin by looking for three ways that God has shown you His love today, and write them down. How have I seen God's hand in my life today? Maybe it's just the sunshine. Maybe it's the fact that I had gas in my car this morning. Maybe someone spoke to me and lifted my spirits. Whatever it might be, really strive to notice the simple little ways that God's love for you is manifest in your life.

One woman in recovery stated:

When I first found out about my husband's pornography addiction, I turned to God for strength. However, as the pain piled upon me and more things came to light, I began to be blinded. I became more and more angry with men and eventually God. I became numb to His spirit and I did not trust Him.

No one at church would have known the difference: I did all the things I should, but I was sad and anxious and angry most of the time. I knew I was lost, and I knew the decrease in my spirituality was to blame, but I did not know how to rekindle that fire I had once had. Reading scriptures, attending church, and praying all left me feeling triggered and furious.

The only thing I could do without anger was counting my blessings. I started by writing three things I was grateful for every night. Slowly I was able to read my scriptures without feeling angry, and eventually I began to feel God's spirit in my daily life again. By noticing what I was grateful for daily, my eyes were opened and I saw clearly how God was and had been supporting me. Now, a few years later, I have a strong, trusting relationship with God again.

What Can I Do About ~~Him?~~ Me?

When we can truly see God's hand in our lives, we are humbled. To us it is proof that He has not forsaken us. He has not left us in our pain, and we can feel safe putting our faith and trust in *Him*. In moments of bitter pain, it may be easy to believe that not only has our husband left us alone to suffer, but that God has too. But if we look daily to see His hand in our lives, we should recognize that it was our eyes that were blinded by pain and fear, leading us to believe He had abandoned us. In reality, He has walked by our side the entire journey.

God's patience with me was amazing, especially at first when I didn't want to accept gratitude as the answer. It's difficult to be grateful in the midst of suffering. When the answer came to count my blessings, I still couldn't see any purpose to my pain. My suffering was unavoidable because of my husband's betrayals, of course, but there came a point when I didn't want to be a victim of my husband's behavior any longer. So I chose to let go of my suffering and to try to be grateful in every circumstance. Feeling like a victim drove me further from gratitude. But as I choose to have gratitude, I take myself out of a victimized place and allow myself to feel joy, and take advantage of the blessings that I do have.

Gratitude is one of the golden keys to healing. Melody Beattie, author of *Codependent No More* and *The Language of Letting Go*, writes:

> *Gratitude unlocks the fullness of life. It turns what we have into enough, and more. It turns denial into acceptance, chaos to order, confusion to clarity. It can turn a meal into a feast, a house into a home, a stranger into a friend. . . . Gratitude makes sense of our past, brings peace for today, and creates a vision for tomorrow.*[36]

No matter what the challenge or difficulty, I can be grateful in the present moment for life itself. Once our suffering finds purpose, we see ourselves being refined through this process, letting go of the victim mindset, and adopting an attitude of gratitude. "Today is a gift; that is why we call it the *present*."

---

36 Melody Beattie, *The Language of Letting Go: A Meditation Book and Journal for Daily Reflection* (Center City, MN: Hazelden Publishing, 2003), August.

What I Can Do

SELF–CARE AND *HIS* CARE

During the long months when I felt so discouraged, I would often buy an inexpensive little bunch of alstroemeria flowers and put them in my kitchen, bathroom, and occasionally in my bedroom where I could see them.

Alstroemeria is not only beautiful but it is one of the most enduring flowers you can buy. These brightly colored flowers with speckled petals get up to two weeks of vase life and are very hardy in cold temperatures. I wanted to be enduring and hardy too. God's flowers, His creations, were a sign that He cared for me and that He knows me.

Alstroemeria are a type of lily, and I think of them as the "poor man's lily." In Luke 12:27, Christ says, "Consider the lilies how they grow: they toil not, they spin not; and yet, I say unto you, that Solomon in all his glory was not arrayed like one of these." The lilies don't work to be cared for by God, they just are. Despite what we may do or how we may feel, the Lord loves us; He tends to all of His creations. A song that spoke to my heart during this time of pain called "Consider the Lilies" references that scripture in Luke. This song says, "And He will heal those who trust Him, and make their hearts as gold."[37] I have felt His love immensely in

---

37 Hoffman, *Consider the Lilies*, 5-6.

the darkest times of my life. Because He loves us and cares for us, we need to care for ourselves as well.

The Importance of Self-Care

Once I understood that I needed to pursue my own recovery, I realized that I did not know how to feel, how to recognize my feelings, or how to express my feelings very well. In my busy and responsible roles as wife, mom, and community servant, I spent much more time becoming what others needed me to be than focusing on my own emotions. I believed that "If Mama ain't happy, ain't nobody happy." I thought that in order to keep everyone happy, I had to keep it together. As women and especially as moms, we seem to have a difficult time taking care of ourselves. We are constantly reacting to whatever is coming at us. We seldom take time to reflect on our own needs because a host of other demands are pulling on us most of the time: children must be bathed, floors must be swept, groceries must be bought, and meals must be cooked. We think we have to keep going even when our own gas tank is on empty.

When trauma enters our lives, however, it is vital to slow down, quiet the craziness, care for ourselves, and regain perspective. We would do well to ask ourselves, "How do I feel?" and "What do I need right now?" We simply must accept that our needs matter, and that God encourages us to take care of our personal feelings and needs. We may even feel selfish when we take time to care for ourselves, but knowing that God loves us no matter what reminds us of the importance of caring for ourselves the way God cares for us.

I often think of the analogy of sharpening a saw. Now, I have used a saw to prune the fruit trees in my yard enough times to know that sawing with a dull saw takes at least twice as long and a lot more energy than if I had just taken a few minutes to sharpen the saw in the first place. But, there I go, pushing and pulling that little rusted saw back and forth, thinking that I really am doing something but making little progress. The whole process would be faster and more productive if I stopped and first took time to "sharpen the saw."[38] So what does sharpening the saw mean for you?

Early in my marriage, I would sometimes call my mother when I was feeling upset, frustrated, or sad. She would listen to me and then say, "Well, go for a walk and get a big drink of water." That was her way of encouraging me to sharpen the saw and care for myself. Every person has different remedies for their sadness and despair, but here are some ideas for self-care that I have developed throughout my recovery process.

Take a Walk

Just go out—this is not an exercise walk. Look around. Focus on other things for a few minutes. Sometimes we think that it's all or nothing, and we tell ourselves that if we can't exercise for an hour and break a good sweat, then it's not worth our time. That often ends in us not doing anything at all. Sometimes when I was in a crisis, all I could do was walk slowly. But to this day, I know that taking a simple walk still does me a great deal of good.

Listen to Soothing Music

Music often gives me solace in my darkest times. Often as I walked, I would sing the simple songs of faith that I had learned as a child. I would sing, "I am happy today for the sunshine, for skies of gray or blue." Now I wasn't really happy, but I was trying to be. And then the song goes on to say, "No cloud can cast a shadow, Over courage such as mine."[39] I was really trying to muster courage. The music and the message reminded me of God's love, and inspired me to take just one more step.

Sometimes music may trigger moments of deep emotion or sadness, from which at first I would try to retreat. But I have realized that it is okay to feel such emotion and work through it. In the midst of trauma, listening to Rachmaninoff's "Rhapsody on a Theme of Paganini" could lift my spirits immensely, or bring out intense feelings of sorrow and enable me to feel and

---

38 Steven R. Covey, *7 Habits of Highly Effective People* (New York: NY, Free Press, 2004).
39 Mr.. and Mrs. N. W. Christiansen, "Happiness," in *Sing with Me: Songs for Children* (Salt Lake City: Deseret Book Company, 1969), G-19.

What Can I Do About ~~Him?~~ *Me?*

cry. Finding music that both uplifts and fills my soul has been a significant aspect of my self-care.

Cry

It's okay to cry. You may need to cry this one out. Go to your knees and surrender to Heavenly Father and ask for His comfort. I have found that tears can be very therapeutic. Victor Frankl said, "There's no need to be ashamed of tears, for tears bear witness that a man has the greatest of courage, the courage to suffer."[40] Crying and feeling sadness can ironically be a positive form of self-care.

Another woman in recovery said:

> *Though I had shut off my tears for years, I began to give myself the assignment: "Write, read, or pray until I cry." ...Otherwise, I knew from experience that the pent-up emotions would just follow me around all day, cutting into my serenity and effectiveness at work, with my children, and in everything I did.*

For me, a good cry happens when I humbly approach God and express the deepest feelings in my heart. In my deepest feelings of despair after Steven's second disclosure, I knelt by my bed and poured out my anguish. I cried and cried and pled with the Lord. As I expressed my grief and my need for comfort, I felt as though a warm blanket was wrapped around my shoulders.

Take a 20-Minute Power Nap

Recognize when you feel tired. If I am tired, I am vulnerable to fear and destructive feelings, and I know I need to take a short 20-minute nap. I set my kitchen timer and I lie on the couch for exactly 20 minutes. It may be difficult to consider taking a nap with little ones running about. However, setting this boundary for yourself can be very beneficial. You might try to fit it in when the kids are having a quiet moment, like nap

---

40 Viktor E. Frankl, *Man's Search for Meaning* (New York: Washington Square Press, 1985), 100.

time or book time. When I get up, even if I didn't actually sleep, I feel surprisingly rejuvenated!

Sleep

A good night's sleep is critical. Seven to eight hours is optimal. Sleep is not the thing to be sacrificing during a time of crisis. Some of us will do anything to distract ourselves from the pain and might spend hours on the internet, in front of the TV, or crafting when it is time to sleep. This is a great disservice to ourselves and others close to us. We need sleep for that is when our bodies and minds repair and heal.

It can be difficult to go to or stay asleep when there is crisis in our lives. Thoughts may swirl through our heads and keep us awake. I have learned a few key strategies when it comes to getting a good night's rest. Decreasing time in front of a TV or computer before bed, decreasing caffeine, and surrendering our fears before bed can all help. Also, if I lay in bed for longer than a half hour I will get up and read a book until I feel sleepy. It is almost impossible to force ourselves to sleep. Interestingly, sleep is another way we learn to surrender.

Eat Well

Feed your mind and your body. Both need fuel—*healthy* fuel. We cannot escape pain by eating too much or too little. When we are in crisis we might feel nauseous or sick about eating. We might even turn to fat or sugar or soda pop to numb bad feelings. For me, the bag of chocolate chips was always calling my name. I justified it because I only ate one handful at a time (unfortunately that added up to about a bag a day). We might also forget to drink an adequate amount of water and become dehydrated. Our minds and bodies function best with an adequate amount of healthy foods (protein and produce). I function best when I eat six small meals a day. Find the right amount for you. I can't emphasize enough the foundational importance of eating appropriately—even if it's in small amounts—and drinking water to keep our minds and bodies healthy during a season of crisis.

What Can I Do About ~~Him?~~ Me?

Make Time for Meditation

I love quiet time. In that time more than any other, I feel God's love. There is so much going on around us constantly that even when we have an opportunity to meditate, we may habitually turn to other things to distract us. Though it might be painful, we need time to think. There will always be other things we need to get done, but time to ponder and to feel should be a top priority, even when it doesn't result in some sort of finished product to check off a list. We are blessed as we accept His invitation to "be still and know that I am God."[41]

We may need to protect that quiet time from our own negative thinking. I had to block certain thoughts like *What if something bad happens?* or *How can I fix this problem?* These thoughts may lead to frustration and fear. My desire for peace turns to anxiety when I go to those places in my mind. During quiet time we can ponder and reflect on our blessings. Most important, we can receive guidance and peace from God in these sacred moments.

Slow Down Your Life

For me, slowing my life down meant quitting something that was taking a lot of my time and effort. At the time of my husband's arrest, I was a student at Brigham Young University. Many things added to the trauma. I had no idea what was going to happen, but I knew I had to quit school for that semester. The extra stress, even for a good cause, was not worth it at that time in my life. I struggled because I wanted to continue towards my goal, and I resented my husband's behavior that was causing me to delay my education. But for my benefit and my children's, I withdrew. It made life much less demanding and hectic. A semester later, when I felt my life was more peaceful, I was able to return to school.

Maybe young moms can simplify by buying a month's supply of paper plates and cups. If you have to feed your children spaghetti or mac and cheese for dinner frequently, do it. I promise it won't stunt their growth if it's for a short time. Tomato soup with grilled cheese sandwiches, or

---

41 D&C 101:16.

scrambled eggs, were staples for my family during times when it seemed I could barely drag myself to the kitchen to fix any food.

Many of us may feel that during times of acute stress, we must continue to act like superwoman and care for the neighbors, the PTA, the church responsibilities, and every child on the block. We must be able to say, "No!" Or at least, "Thank you for asking, but I am not able to do that right now." No other explanation is necessary. (I haven't mastered this—yet.)

Because of the trauma we've suffered, we are sick. When we are in the hospital emotionally, we need to allow ourselves to be in healing mode. If you've just had a heart attack, you probably won't be able to get up, fold up the sheets and start doing the laundry the same day. Simple acts of service to those in our family, especially our children, may be all that we can give in such a time of crisis. Basic needs should be the priority. Extra responsibilities will have to wait.

Don't Compare Yourself

In the early years of my marriage, I felt that I wasn't good enough. Then I found out that I had a husband who was viewing pornography and going to strip clubs, which only seemed to confirm my inadequacy. With every glossy magazine ad and lingerie commercial on TV or in a magazine I would think, *Wow, I just don't compare.* Now, in recovery, I recognize that nobody can compare to the falseness of television or manipulated content in other media. Comparing ourselves to others in any way—looks, intelligence, or ability—is dangerous. When we compare, we think of ourselves as either less than or better than. It is not uncommon for women to respond to their husband's pornography addiction by trying to dramatically change their bodies by crash diets or unnecessary plastic surgeries. Some will try nearly anything to control their husband's behaviors and meet society's false standard of attractiveness. Beware that such responses can destroy us, both physically and emotionally.

Beyond physical beauty, we also risk negative outcomes when we compare our talents and abilities. One of my friends once called to talk through her frustration about not having time to get everything done. She was dealing with a part-time job and a new baby, all while working on her own recovery and working with her husband to recover their marriage. She couldn't figure out how to get the house cleaning all done. Well, come to find out, she had just spent quite a bit of time on a web site with marvelous ideas about how to keep your house spotless and also find time to make cute cards, aprons, and matching lamp shades. She was comparing herself to women she did not know, assuming that they had it all together. She asked me how often I thought the refrigerator needed to be cleaned. I responded, "When it starts to grow." The next question was, "When do you clean the blinds?" My response was, "When you can't see out the windows." We started to laugh. It didn't take long for us to realize that it would be best for her to take her cleaning spreadsheet, fold it up very neat and small, and drop it in her surrender box!

When I was a young mom with three little children, I had a friend who vacuumed her carpets three times a day. With that kind of standard to compare to, I would never be an adequate housekeeper. But I did have other abilities, and I used them. Fortunately, my children didn't seem to suffer because of my once-a-week vacuuming practice.

Over time I've embraced who I am—feeling at peace with myself from the inside. My self-worth doesn't depend on what anyone thinks of me. In fact, it is none of my concern what anyone else thinks of me. I choose to acknowledge my self-worth. That's both vital and difficult, so I still work on it.

I try to be the best that I can be. I put some makeup on and do my hair to feel good about myself. I make an effort, but it's definitely not to please my husband; it's so I am true to the best in me. In this sexualized world, there are countless women who feel inadequate in comparison to those airbrushed images most have seen. So much of this deception can be resolved by asking, "Am I loved by God?" If I can reply, "I am cherished by the most powerful Being in the universe, and He knows me and loves me," then I am enough. I am a beloved daughter of God, and I am responsible to care for myself. Once I recognize this, I will care for myself physically, emotionally, and spiritually, and I will feel His sustaining influence.

Do Something Just for You

What can you do just for you? It might be something pampering such as soaking in a bubble bath. It might be an escape to the library by yourself. None of these things need be extravagant, lengthy, or expensive. Find something that pleases you deeply. Consider carefully whether such activities are reinforcing pain or freeing you from pain. Excessive shopping or internet surfing may be more self-medicating than self-care. I have to take into account my motivation to find something that fills my soul rather than something that just fills my time.

I have found an example of how to fill my soul in my young grandchildren. They truly live in the present by running, playing, and expressing their love openly to me. I have tried to be more childlike in that way. I love to swing, so I suggest to friends who need self-care to go to the nearest park and swing for a while. Feeling the air rush by me, the sun warming my face, and the freedom of movement helps me appreciate the gift of the present moment.

Be Present

Early in my marriage I became an avid planner. I was convinced that if I were well organized, with planner in hand, I would be a better wife and mother. I was the doer, the *über*-responsible one. Organization and planning have their place, but I was so tied to my plan that I constantly focused on the next task and fretted over how I would get it all done.

Since then, I've discovered that my life is unmanageable on my own. Instead of running about with an overflowing planner under my arm, I try to be where my feet are. Worrying about what I must do tomorrow, or brooding about whether I said just the right thing yesterday, robs me of the wonderful gift of the present. Resentments from the past and what-ifs of the future tend to paralyze me.

It may sometimes be difficult to see the blessings of the present moment. When I recognize that I have been blind to blessings before my eyes, I start to list the my most simple blessings—such as a roof over my head (even if I'm uncertain how long that might last), adequate food in the refrigerator, sunshine, a warm rain, or a garage to keep snow off my car. This causes my perspective to shift.

I am now more present when my children and grandchildren come to visit, and I do not feel guilty if there are no homemade cookies coming out of the oven. (Popcorn will do.) I sit and look into the faces of my family members and really listen. I can feel the present.

Write in Your Journal

Writing down my feelings has been great therapy. Early on in my efforts of recovery, I wrote letters to my husband—in my journal. I wrote to him about sadness. "I am sad that I can't fully trust you, that I haven't been able to trust you for most of our marriage. I am sad that we have lost so much time, time that we could have been fulfilling our dreams."

I also wrote about resentment. "I resent your selfish attitude, seeing only what you wanted and not considering others' needs, especially your family's. I resent the times that you wouldn't come to help me or be with the family because you had so much to do at work or you had another trip to go on, and all the time you were wasting trying to satisfy your sexual addiction."

This is painful material, so you may want to use a new or separate journal, one that you can safely vent all your feelings in—even the ugly ones. There may come a time when you will want to burn that journal as a symbol of letting go of those feelings, but that moment will come in its own due time.

Eighteen months into my own recovery, I re-read my journals from 20 years before. I was devastated as I was reminded about the efforts I had made to change myself and my marriage—without knowing the truth. I was overcome with grief and relapsed into feeling like a victim. So it may be wise to keep such journals closed while you work your initial steps of recovery.

In addition to this kind of writing therapy, I also kept a separate "gratitude journal" in which I wrote about the small things I was grateful for each day. What a blessing it has been! I'm grateful for the times when I have been able to write about wonderful, happy days. Keeping both kinds of journals has provided an outlet to express my feelings more openly.

Study Your Scriptures and Pray

These are essential. If you can only do two things right now, make it scripture study and prayer. I began writing dates next to verses that were direct answers to my questions. So whenever I felt overwhelmed, these special scriptures gave me something tangible to always go back to. Here are some that have guided me the most.

Isaiah 58:11 *"And the Lord shall guide thee continually, and satisfy thy soul."*

Mark 11:24 *"What things soever ye desire, when ye pray, believe that ye receive them, and ye shall have them."*

1 Peter 3:15 *"But sanctify the Lord God in your hearts: and be ready always to give an answer to every man that asketh you a reason of the hope that is in you with meekness and fear [reverence]."*

These scriptures and many others have given me hope, courage, and purpose to my life—all things that I need to move forward.

Prayer, for me, is any form of communication with God. I am on my knees each morning and night and frequently in between, but I also have other ways of communicating with my Father. I often find myself sending up a prayer of need or gratitude while I am driving and it is quiet in the car. Some women I know who have lost communication with God for years, choose to start by writing letters to God expressing their pain, anger, gratitude, and love.

Singing or humming a hymn or spiritual song is a form of prayer when I don't have the words to express my feelings. On the morning of September 11, 2001, while driving my twin sons to school, we heard about the attack on the World Trade Center. We were shocked and terrified. As we rode in stunned silence all I could do was sing, and my twelve-year-old sons sang along: "Fear not, though the enemy deride; Courage, for the

Lord is on our side. We will heed not what the wicked may say, But the Lord alone we will obey."[42] We sang it with courage and with tears in our eyes as a prayer to our God.

Dailies

It is not expected that we implement all of these suggestions right away. But it can be calming in seasons of chaos to do certain things every day. I give my life some degree of order by working on these select tasks every day. These are called "dailies."

I often ask women in crisis how they are doing physically, emotionally, and spiritually. During one such check-in by phone, I spoke with a woman who was very down. I was impressed to ask, "Have you had anything to eat this morning?" She said, "No." "Have you gotten dressed?" Again, the answer was "No." I responded, "Okay, let's go step by step. Go get something nutritious to eat—some protein and fruit. Then get dressed. Then call me again. We will go from there." On some difficult days, that may be all we can do. We can only see a couple of steps in front of us. So we should say to ourselves, *I'll take this step first, and then I'll find out what I should do next.*

One woman working recovery said, "Dailies help calm and ease our minds through focusing on that daily. They help take us out of our fear, obsession, or anger cycles. When we take care of ourselves we are controlling what we can and releasing what we can't."

I realize that it's much more difficult to slow down and go on a walk, or take a short nap, when we have a house full of little kids. But if I could go back to the time I had seven little children at home, I would take such time to care for my needs. It would have made me a better and calmer mom.

Much of our self-care is fostering God's love for us, and trusting that God will take care of us when we've done all we can. Doing all we can consists most often of simple and small steps to care for ourselves. Although we may have held the opinion that to care for ourselves is selfish,

---

42 Evan Stephens, "Let Us All Press On," in *Hymns of The Church of Jesus Christ of Latter-day Saints* (Salt Lake City: The Church of Jesus Christ of Latter-day Saints, 2002), 243.

it is not. Caring for ourselves expresses our appreciation to God by our careful stewardship of His creation—life.

What I Can Do

I'LL ROW MY OWN BOAT

After Steven came forward the third time with his addiction, our middle son brought us a painting that had been given to him and his wife. He felt that it was applicable to his dad's situation. That painting is titled "Gently Up the Stream." It depicts two individuals in separate boats paddling up a tranquil river. I have imagined that one is a woman and the other is a man. In my mind this painting represents my marriage; we are in separate boats, but we are hopefully headed in the same direction—together. Farther up the stream is a beautiful, beckoning light; below is an unseen drop to certain destruction.

The artist, Linda Curley Christensen, said this regarding the symbolism in her painting:

> *If life is compared to a river, it is easy to imagine floating with* the current, gently down *the stream; but I have never found any good and worthwhile thing that came of its own accord—just the opposite. Every worthy goal takes constant, if gentle, effort.... Fortunately, the Lord does not require us to run [or paddle] faster than we have strength.*[43]

---

43 Linda Curley Christensen, "Gently Up the Stream: Artist Statement," The Art of Linda Curley Christensen, http://lindacurley.com/originals.php?id=102.

What Can I Do About ~~Him?~~ Me?

Rowing Gently

Anything of worth requires effort, but we don't have to work extraordinarily hard in order to make that effort. You don't have to frantically beat the water! We just have to row gently *up* the stream to be safe and succeed. At first, you're going to have to make a concerted effort because you might be close to the edge of that falls. It may be hard work to paddle away from the devastating rocks that await at the bottom of the waterfall. However, at a certain point it gets easier and all you have to do is just keep paddling. Gently.

Sharing the Boat

Early in my marriage, I believed that my husband and I were in the same boat. It was a lovely feeling, thinking that we were this connected union—loving, working, and going in the same direction. These were part of my romantic views of what a marriage is supposed to be. My husband was supposed to be the head of the household. And besides, if I took over the boat, I would have to be accountable for everything, even the mistakes I would make. But I was in his boat, eager to just look the other way; and I was merrily—but not as strongly—rowing from the back.

A few years into our marriage and several children later, I discovered that when my husband was traveling I could handle the family pretty well; I would really grab on to the oars. But as soon as he was back in town, I would let go and expect him to take over. My expectations often created resentment and frustration when he didn't take over the way that I thought he should. I still wanted him to be back at the helm of our boat, but I tended to nudge him repeatedly with my oar, asking him to get it together.

At other times, I played the rescuer. I wanted to put everyone in my boat and row for them (or as I had perceived it at the time, my handcart). As a wife and a mother, I wanted to be loving, kind, and of service, but I've learned with that comes a tendency to control. When I tried to row for everyone that I love, I generally ended up resenting the hard work, and they resented me for interfering with their choices. Certainly young children need our guidance, but as our children mature they know innately that they have their own choices to make, their own boats to row.

I was not aware before I started recovery that the only way to make it up stream to that beautiful goal ahead is to be in our own boat. Each one of us has to make our own choices on that voyage.

One experience, which happened years before I knew anything about recovery, illustrates this principle. When my sixth child, the next to the last son, was 16, he began to push back and want to do things his own way. After parenting four teenage boys, I have learned that you really can't force them; they have to do some things their own way. Even though I have learned this lesson time and time again, I still gave into my habit to control.

My son was getting a bad midterm grade in band. We are a musical family, so there's a lot of shame if you're getting a bad grade in band! When I saw that, I reacted. Over breakfast I told him that he was going to fail band, that he was never going to get a scholarship, and besides, how could he be successful in college if he couldn't manage a passing grade in band?

He started to get tears in his eyes, and I quickly realized that I had crossed a boundary with my need to control. I felt terrible and knew I was in the wrong. It was no longer about his bad grade in band, it was about my behavior. He left for school still with tears in his eyes, and he and his brother did not give me their usual hug and expression of love as they left. I soon got on my knees, where I prayed and asked forgiveness.

I wrote an apology on a card, called the high school, and asked that he be checked out so that I could take him to lunch. When I arrived he was slouched down as he waited for me, which was not usual demeanor. I was saddened again because that fallen countenance was my doing. On our way to lunch he didn't say a thing. Once we started eating I said, "I am so sorry. I want to apologize for trying to force you, and making you feel bad."

I gave him the card and he read my note. I quietly asked, "Can you forgive me?"

His slow and wavering response was, "I don't know."

Hearing that broke my heart, and my eyes brimmed with tears.

What Can I Do About ~~Him?~~ Me?

Then he said, "Do you remember, Mom, in one of the church talks we learned about trying to lead a horse? If you pull him, he won't go. But if you walk beside him, he'll walk with you. Mom. Please. Just *walk beside me.*"

I was stunned. My 16-year-old son was teaching me how to relinquish control. That simple statement taught me an invaluable lesson and has become a guiding principle ever since.

In My Own Boat

In the past, I thought it was my duty to "encourage" my loved ones to succeed. I thought I was encouraging, but in reality I was controlling. After hitting my own rock bottom, I have acknowledged that we should not control or force or push or pull. That's not the way our Heavenly Father governs us. He gives us commandments and allows us to choose what path we will take. Once we choose, we receive blessings or consequences based on our choices.

Specifically for spouses of an addict, we should understand and accept these three elements for our own recovery:

1. We are not responsible for his addiction—it is not our fault.

2. We cannot fix his addiction.

3. We cannot control his addiction.

As my young son taught me a few years ago, we should *walk beside* our loved ones in their path to recovery. It is not our fault, we cannot fix it, nor can we control it. All we can do is row our own boats gently up the stream, with our eyes focused ahead and upward, and an occasional glance to the side to see if he is continuing to row in the same direction.

When I say "I'll row my own boat," I am not referring to being defiantly self-sufficient. Of course I deeply care if my loved ones are rowing their own boats toward a good destination. I love them. Such attachment in close relationships is essential for every human being. So when I say "I row my own boat," I mean I take accountability for my own actions, and

I allow others to make their own choices and take accountability for their own actions.

I remember one experience of a woman I worked closely with in her recovery. Her husband said to her, "Fix my soul." She told me later:

> *I had engaged in supporting that crazy belief, by my trying to be the perfect one, the peacemaker, the "glue that keeps our family together." I came to the realization that only a Higher Power, a Savior, could "fix" anyone's soul, and by trying to fix my husband, I had been trying to assume the role of savior. Wow.*

Like this woman, I, too, have come to the realization that I cannot control my husband's sexual addiction. In a meeting with our therapist, I once made the comment that I didn't feel like my husband loved me. He responded, "He doesn't! He can't. He doesn't love anybody; he's not capable of it in his addiction." As difficult as it was for me to hear this, it was freeing. It helped me realize that it's not about *me*. I have my faults, but this is not about me. I cannot make him change. I cannot make him love me. One thing I can do is make sure I am gently rowing my own boat *up* the stream.

Courage to Row in the Face of Fear

I have had a persistent fear of swimming in deep water, since my childhood. I know what it's like to thrash about in the water worried that I am going to die and wondering if I'll ever breathe again. It's interesting, then, to imagine myself rowing my own boat through deep and turbulent water, because as you can imagine, water is a terrifying place for me to be. I think it describes well how challenging it has been for me to row my own boat. I naturally associate fear with the "water," and overcoming fear has been a key element to understand how to row my own boat.

When I was in college in my fifties, trying to keep up with the homework, tests, and papers, I ran into one of my professors one day and he asked, "How are you doing?"

I said, "Oh, I'm just keeping my head above water."

He replied, "Don't."

"What?" I asked. *What did he mean, <u>don't</u> keep my head above water? I'll drown! I'll fail!*

"No, just relax."

That was all he said. He saw something in me that I did not see in myself. He saw me panicking, thrashing about and trying to keep my head above water. Basically he was saying, "Relax. God will take care of you."

Through my recovery, I have discovered that I can row my own boat, but I have stopped thrashing around like I'm going to die. I'm going to learn how to do this with faith and motivation.

The River of Recovery

Along with our fear, sometimes we are discouraged when recovery does not come as quickly as we want. Most of us tend to be impatient with ourselves and with other people. We want our problems fixed *now,* and we want the process to be easy so that we can quickly return to "normal" life.

About three years ago I started to exercise in earnest. Oh, I had made valiant short-term efforts when I was younger, but they never seemed to last for more than a few weeks or months. Back then I wanted to be fit, but I wanted it to be easy and immediate. Not until I reached my late fifties did I hit rock bottom and realize that if I didn't take care of my health, I might lose it.

At this age exercising was painful, and I wondered if I could do it or even if I wanted to continue. But I kept going week after week and it started to get a bit easier. Now I look forward to exercising—several times a week. I no longer have to drag myself to exercise; instead I feel proud of myself in the strength I have built.

Just like my experience with exercise, doing the work of recovery and rowing my own boat seemed nearly impossible at times, and I really didn't want to do it. Why did I have to row? After all, it was his problem that had caused so much grief. At first it was exhausting labor. But as I kept working—one day, one stroke at a time—I got further and further away from the rapids of resentment, bitterness, self-pity, and blame that threatened to destroy me. Now my goal is to just gently row and enjoy the beautiful scenery.

The more I recover and heal, and the more I work the principles of healthy living, the less effort I have to make in rowing. I no longer beat the water to death. If I row gently, I continue to move forward and progress. What propels me up the stream? Trusting in God, taking care of myself, practicing gratitude, and setting and maintaining boundaries—that is how I row. It might be a slow stroke, but I still continue gently up the stream. It may seem that the power comes from our own arms, but I have discovered that I am not all that strong on my own. Only my trust in God and His power can move me forward in my goal to find healing and recovery.

What I Can Do

AND THEY LIVED HAPPILY...
ONE DAY AT A TIME

Years ago I saw a beautiful pillow on which was printed, "They lived happily ever after." That's of course one of those fairy tale statements that we all just think is *wonderful*. But at the point of my life when I read that, I was more skeptical than ever. I nursed some deep resentments about my dream of living happily ever after because the dragon had conquered the prince, and I was a damsel left in distress.

As I have worked on my own recovery, I have discovered that I can be happy for one minute, or ten minutes, or one day at a time—if I so choose. So as I sit and think about that beautiful pillow, all fancy, I think, *I want a pillow for my bed that says, "And they lived happily . . . one day at a time."* That is all we have! There is no guarantee of happily ever after. That truly is a fairy tale. But happily one day at a time?—that's available to each of us.

On my own path of recovery, I have learned to gird myself with my own armor and wield my own sword. As one author writes, "Redeemed women of God have tender merciful hearts, backbones of steel, and hands that are prepared for the fight."[44] This is the kind of woman I want to be. As women,

---

44 John and Stasi Eldredge, *Captivating: Unveiling the Mystery of a Woman's Soul* (Nashville: Thomas Nelson Publishing, 2005), 190.

What Can I Do About ~~Him?~~ Me?

we may naturally have tender, merciful hearts; however, backbones of steel and hands that are prepared for the fight require training and practice in order to successfully fight the dragon of evil for the benefit of our homes and families.

Even though my heart has been broken at times, I want to retain a tender merciful heart—the kind of heart that is vulnerable, open to all emotions, and engaged in honest, intimate relationships. If my heart is hardened, no matter what the cause, I cannot live to my fullest potential.

Gaining and maintaining a backbone of steel has proven to be a difficult task for me. By setting and holding emotional, physical, and spiritual boundaries and standing up with courageous determination to do what I know to be right, I continue to forge my backbone of steel.

Possessing "hands that are prepared for the fight" is wonderful imagery.[45] As women, I believe that we want to fight against evil, and we have power greater than we've ever imagined to aid us in that fight. I have heard women leaders who speak with such power, passion, and courage that I want to stand up, raise my hand, and shout, "Count me in!"

I believe that one of the most devastating evil plagues of our day is pornography and sexual addiction. It is the one thing that is destroying more families than any other. All women, including myself, have the right to fight against this enemy. Whether it is within our own families or within our community, we can combat sexual addiction and know that we are doing God's work. I want to do what I believe is God's will for me, and I believe that every good woman wants to do the same.

A few months ago we sat as a family—all of our children, their spouses, and 14 grandchildren—around a warm campfire on a beautiful summer night. My husband played his guitar as we all sang the old standbys and our favorite Beatle's song, "Love You Forever." I had three sleepy little granddaughters snuggled into my lap, and life could not have been better. I chose in that moment—and many since—to feel, to love, and to be vulnerable.

I no longer need a guarantee of happiness for tomorrow, for if I worry about what might happen, I might rob myself of the priceless gift of the

---

[45] Ibid.

present. I don't have to survive in a state of fear because I can surrender to my God. I enjoy a more authentic relationship with God assured that He loves me, He knows me, and He will continue to guide my life.

My willingness to be vulnerable and surrender my life to God, is miraculously—and unexpectedly—the secret to my empowerment and serenity. This may be the greatest paradox of recovery, and raises the question, "How can it be?"

The answer lies in acquiring the courage to change the things I can change—the courage to do something about *ME*.

I know you can do this, too.

What I Can Do

Appendix

MAKING THE DECISION

By Steven Croshaw

My first impression of Rhyll when I met her 40 years ago was right: she loves God, has incredible grit, is wonderfully talented, and is beautiful both on the inside and the outside. Her grace and power is evident in all she is and does as a daughter of God, wife, mother, grandmother, friend, and mentor. I am grateful and incredibly blessed that she has been willing to walk the difficult pathway of recovery beside me. Had she not had faith in God and a belief in His grace, she could not and would not have been able to meet the challenges I brought upon her because of my lies and betrayal related to my sexual addiction. I love her and thank God each day for my marriage to her.

My behaviors associated with sexual addiction were extremely selfish. For decades I was willing to risk all that was dear to me for brief moments of pleasure. For reasons that are impossible to make sense of, I was exchanging diamonds for a "bowl of pottage." I chose to practice the ways of the adversary. I pulled away emotionally and spiritually from God, Rhyll, and my family. The stark truth of my self-centered behaviors is ugly and painful to recall—let alone write about and share with the world. Nevertheless, I have chosen to tell my story publicly in an effort to help others who may be seeking recovery in their own lives.

A most important part of telling my story is to first acknowledge the immense pain and deep trauma that I alone have caused in the lives of those I am committed to love and protect most. My actions were the direct opposite of what they should have been as a man, husband, and father. Rhyll has suffered the pain and trauma of betrayal over decades of our marriage. She has gone through her own Gethsemane, suffering because of my choices—not hers. I have apologized countless times, but apologies are far too insignificant to even begin to make amends for my lies, deceit, and betrayals. I recognize that my actions must include not only working my own recovery, but thoughtfully supporting Rhyll in her efforts of healing from the wounds I have caused.

To be completely honest, I have struggled to always remember that Rhyll needs my support and understanding daily as she works her own recovery. There are times when I am lax, impatient, or fail to quickly acknowledge my faults. Nevertheless, I can honestly say that my heart is in the effort of working my own recovery and in supporting Rhyll in her healing. I am committed to daily living a life free from the behaviors of sexual addiction, and in being honest. I am looking forward, with an attitude that God's grace is working both in my life and in Rhyll's.

For much of our life together, Rhyll has said that she did not feel much of an emotional connection between us. She was right. She could not feel such a connection because I was emotionally unavailable. Immoral, addictive behaviors, and the resulting shame and lies, as well as the hypocrisy of living a double life, smothered my emotional availability.

Seven years ago, I made a solemn commitment to myself and to God that I wanted recovery from sexual addiction. I was willing to do whatever it might take to truly change. I decided to be unconditionally honest—no matter what the consequences. At the darkest point in my life, I finally surrendered and decided to be honest with myself, God, Rhyll, and my family. I made a decision to put myself in God's hands.

My Interruption and Spiritual Awakening

My path of recovery began with willingness and a softened heart. But my heart was not softened until I was abruptly awakened by a significant interruption to my pattern of behavior. On August 25, 2005, when I was arrested for picking up a prostitute, I thought my life had ended. Yet, in reality, my life of recovery was just beginning.

I fervently believe that God's hand was mercifully involved in my arrest. It was a curious experience. That day, I had no time and I had no money. In fact, I didn't intend to act out with the prostitute. But I was presented with an opportunity, and so I picked up a girl with the intent of driving around the block and then letting her off. I often wonder, *Why did I do that? I had no time or money.* If I'm honest with myself, I did it because I wanted a "lust hit."

The next day when I met with an attorney to ask what course I should take, I learned that I could likely get the Class B Misdemeanor dismissed. At first I thought, *I've escaped again!* But the cold reality was that I had not escaped. I could not escape myself. In the days that followed my meeting with the attorney, I could not escape from the intensifying pain of the lies, the deceit, the betrayal, and the hypocrisy that I was living.

Getting arrested was a blessing from God. It caused me to seriously contemplate my circumstances. Due to the shock of this interruption, I became willing to soften my heart and made a decision that has altered the course of my life. When I needed Him the most, He was there. He had, of course, been there the whole time, but I was finally ready to accept Him into my life, into my battered, and now softened, heart.

Making the Decision

Making the decision to come forward for the third time was the most difficult and spiritual experience of my life. On the night of September 11, 2005, I lay in bed awake all night worrying about both the mess I was in and about being found out. As I lay there pondering my situation, I began to consider my belief in God. It was overwhelmingly powerful to candidly ask myself, *Do I believe in God?* I sincerely pondered the question at length. I could only answer, *Yes.* I knew that I believed, and I knew that God knew that I believed. This was a defining moment. It opened up a corner of my dark soul to the sunlight of honesty. It warmed my heart—and tore my insides apart.

The more I contemplated that question and my undeniable answer, the more I realized the degree of the hypocrisy I was living. I was living a double life, and both were loaded with deceit. As I weighed the possible consequences of disclosing my behaviors again, I was filled with fear, shame, inadequacy, and self-loathing. Living one way in secret and presenting myself publicly in another way was difficult, but finally recognizing that I was fearing man more than God motivated me to make the right decision. Even though I was filled with fear, I recognized that I had no choice but to come forward—even if it meant losing my wife and my family. I could no longer carry the unbearable weight of the double life of hypocrisy.

As I look back, the most important decision I have ever made in my life was very early that Sunday morning, September 11, 2005. I resolutely decided that I would come forward and be honest with God, Rhyll, and my family. I could not seriously consider any other options; I simply knew that I had to come forward. So I committed that I would confess to Rhyll and my spiritual leader by nine o'clock that morning that I had relapsed, and had hidden my behaviors from them for the last seven years. I decided to come out of hiding.

When I made that decision, I knew that I had made it in my heart because my fear diminished dramatically, and feelings of "can do—must do" began to increase. I felt the hand of God and His love for me once I made that decision to be honest.

Disclosure to Rhyll, A Spiritual Leader, and My Family

My decision to speak to my spiritual leader by a specific time was important. It was Sunday morning, and our family had gone to church as usual. I procrastinated until five minutes before nine o'clock and knew I was running out of time. I sat on the church bench, uncomfortably waiting for our church leader to arrive. When he finally came in, the only thing I could say was, "I need to speak with you after this meeting."

Rhyll then came into the chapel and sat down next to me. The only thing I said to her was, "I won't be taking the sacrament today; I need to speak with you after church." She immediately knew, as did my church leader, that something was seriously wrong. What I had said seemed sufficient to open the door to my being honest. This was merely the beginning, but I had opened the door and now there was no turning back. As I sat there, I could sense that Rhyll was in deep distress. I was the cause of that pain and

Making the Decision

wished there was something I could do to comfort her. But I could not do a thing. I was angry at myself, guilty of betraying and hurting Rhyll and my family. But there was nothing more I could do at that time—it was now in God's hands. Having not slept the night before I felt tired and numb, and the world seemed a bit blurry. Yet I remained resolute to following through on my commitment to fully disclose.

That afternoon, Rhyll and I met with our church leader. Meeting with him provided the opportunity for a powerful spiritual experience. I had asked Rhyll to go with me and I was grateful she had agreed. I was determined to make an honest, full confession. We arrived at his office and sat down, and he pulled his own chair directly in front of me with our knees almost touching; Rhyll sat to my side.

I began by sharing my earliest recollection of exposure to pornography, and then divulged my entire experience of immoral behaviors. A lifetime of immorality takes some time to confess. It was not as difficult to disclose everything as I thought it might have been because I did not desire to measure or minimize my confession. I stated each fact in chronological order while he intently listened, focused on both my words and the Spirit speaking to his heart.

After I finished my complete and lengthy disclosure, he simply asked, "Do you believe in Jesus Christ and the power of His grace to heal?" I believed in that Power of Grace because I could feel it right then, throughout my body, throughout my being. I did believe, and I knew it.

Little more was said, and our leader explained that he would soon get back to me. He did not promise immediate forgiveness nor that the pathway of repentance would be easy, but I felt profound hope and faith for a healing I had not thought possible the night before. I am forever grateful for the experience of a true and honest confession.

I am very sorry to say I don't remember much of what was said to Rhyll. She was asked about her feelings and if there was anything she needed at the time. I was so wrapped up in my own feelings of guilt and the stress of the day that I was not sensitive to the trauma she was experiencing. As I think about my efforts of recovery during this experience and many others, there was much more I should have and could have done to ease her burdens.

I was slow to grasp the importance of supporting Rhyll in every possible way I could. I can't row her boat for her, but I must not throw water in her boat or do anything that might impede her progress. Recovery has since improved my sensitivity, for which I am grateful. Addictive behavior is very selfish and self-centered; recovery behavior is empathetic and attentive to others.

I have remained on the pathway of honesty from that memorable day forward. That day included a full disclosure to my church leader, Rhyll, and my children. What a challenging experience—yet one of the most powerful in my life. The term "bitter–sweet" comes to mind. Rhyll was numb and said little; my daughters cried; my sons were angry; and my children-in-law were taken aback. I felt as if I was opening up an old festering wound, but one that had to be cleaned out.

That cleaning process caused enormous pain to Rhyll and each member of my family. I was pained as I watched them suffer. I was sorrowful that my wife and children were experiencing such agony, which I had caused. Nevertheless, I was convinced that there was no other pathway; the deep-rooted wounds had to be opened and cleaned before they could properly heal. I accepted that each of us had to go through pain to become whole.

It is amazing to consider what can be accomplished in a day once the decision is made to be honest, humble, and accountable. By making the decision at 3:00 a.m. Sunday morning to come forward and be honest, I set myself on a pathway of recovery. By 11:00 p.m. that night I had spoken to my spiritual leader, Rhyll, and each of our children. My lies, deceit, and betrayal had all been disclosed. And then came hope. And all in one day.

Consulting a Qualified Therapist

It seems that God's hand is always at my shoulder as I take responsibility for my own recovery. For example, He helped me find the qualified counseling I desperately needed. I determined that I would speak with my brother, Alan, and be open with him about where I was in my life. Alan gave me a brochure for a counseling organization he was aware of. I needed to find a qualified therapist, and the information in that brochure led me to an exceptional counselor who, I believe, was instrumental in helping us save our marriage. I don't believe that things like this happen by chance.

Qualified counseling was vital for me at this time. I needed a better understanding of what was going on in my life. A simple brochure given to me at a critical crossroad by someone who loved me didn't just come by chance. Without delay I called the counselor listed in the brochure and set up an appointment, and asked Rhyll to go with me. She responded flatly, "Okay, I'll go."

So we went. I was hopeful and prayerful that something positive would happen. And the most amazing thing did happen in this first meeting. I unfolded my rather lengthy story to the therapist, and he listened patiently and said little. After I had finished, he didn't comment on what I had shared. Instead he looked at Rhyll and pointedly asked, "Can you stay with your husband if he is in recovery?"

The question seemed to take Rhyll by surprise, and her answer showed her confusion: "How could I know if this man were in recovery? He has lied to me over and over for decades. I don't see how I can ever trust him again. How could I possibly know if he were in recovery? I don't even know what recovery looks like." The therapist's simple yet confident response was, "You will know."

I was confused as well, because I didn't know what recovery looked like either. I didn't know what recovery felt like. I don't think I had ever really been in recovery to that point. Considering all this confusion, it is amazing that the therapist would be so bold as to ask, "Can you stay with your husband if he is in recovery?"

That interchange is all I really remember of our first discussion with the therapist. But it is also what I remember most vividly of all of our discussions with the therapist. Todd Olson, our therapist, who is expertly qualified in treating sexual addiction, was instrumental in giving both Rhyll and me a sense of hope about the possibility of recovery in our lives.

At first, we attended counseling together, once a week for an hour, where the discussion was always open and honest. Looking back, it almost seems as though nothing profound was ever discussed, yet valuable insights were taught regarding what recovery takes, and the importance of honesty, accountability, communication, and emotional connection.

One of the greatest realizations I witnessed through our counseling was the unfolding drama in our relationship and communication. I had learned well, how to play the pathetic role of victim. But working with a qualified therapist helped me understand my own challenges as a sexual addict; I was not a victim, for I had made every choice on my own. And, just as important, he helped me understand the incredible challenges that my wife faced because of the trauma that I had brought upon her through my years of dishonesty, deceit, and betrayal. I feel that Rhyll and I working with the same therapist was very influential in my recovery, in her healing, and in rescuing our marriage.

Working a 12-Step Program

One of the most crucial principles of recovery is becoming involved with a 12-Step fellowship. I believe that God's hand guided me in my effort to find a good 12-Step group. Again, my brother's influence was key in this search. He told me where I could find a 12-Step group that was attended by a number of men with long-standing recovery. Even though the meeting was held nearly 60 miles from my home, I resolved that I would attend this meeting every week without fail.

The first time that I went to the 12-Step meeting, I had some fear—fear that I might see someone I knew, fear that I wouldn't know what to say, fear that I was going to be out of place. All of these feelings of anxiety pressed down hard on me, and caused me to ask, *Do I really need to do this?* But deep down I knew that I needed to go, and so I went.

That decision—both to go and to participate—has been one of the most significant actions that I have taken in my recovery. In my first meeting, I met a man who had a story similar to mine and I was amazed. He had had several years of sobriety, seemed genuinely happy, and was positive about life. As I heard his story and felt his love and compassion, I gained a measure of hope from his experience that I also could find recovery.

I have discovered by attending 12-Step meetings faithfully each week—sometimes multiple times a week—that the experience, strength, and hope shared by others who attend has been nothing less than essential in my recovery. Even the social aspect of being part of a 12-Step group is positive and uplifting.

A 12-Step program (often just called "12-Step" for convenience) is a simplified process of recovery and repentance: 12-Step emphasizes key principles, such as the necessity of recognizing my own faults and character weaknesses; having a willingness to admit these faults to others; coming to know God; and having a willingness to ask God to forgive me. Other principles include the importance of admitting my faults immediately to myself; staying in touch with God; and understanding the need to help others. The 12-Step program is very simple, yet very powerful. I am convinced it is inspired.

One of the most significant concepts I learned about sexual addiction as I attended 12-Step meetings, is that ironically, sexual addiction isn't really about sex. It seems a bit strange, but it's true. Sexual addiction is a response to emotional needs, which are spiritual but which are misdirected and driven by lust. The addiction is spiritual, as well as emotional and physical. Lust drives it. The 12-Step program I work, and the meetings I attend, help me gain such critical knowledge that is foundational to my recovery.

There is a great lesson to be understood by all who would seek recovery from sexual addiction. That is:

> *"the program doesn't tell [me] how to stop—[I] had done that a thousand and one times—it shows [me] how to keep from starting again. [I] had it backwards; before, [I] always wanted the therapist, spouse, or God to do the stopping for [me]—to fix [me]. Now [I] stop; and then, in [my] surrender, the power of God becomes effective in [me]."*[46]

In 12-Step I learned the simple definition of *sobriety*: "No sex with self or anyone other than my spouse, and progressive victory over lust." I

---

46 Sexaholics Anonymous, *The White Book*: SA Literature, 2002.

was grateful to have a standard, a point of measurement that covered not only the obvious acts but also the precursors that lead up to acting out. "Progressive victory over lust" included not going to pornography to escape or medicate myself. Therefore, I cannot invite any form of pornography and still consider myself as having progressive victory over lust.

By working 12-Step, I have also learned this basic truth: *sobriety* is not *recovery*. Nevertheless, sobriety is important and is required before I can truly be on the path of recovery.

Surrender: We Win By Giving Over Each Time

Another important lesson that I have learned in 12-Step has taken me years to understand: it is the power of surrender. Attending a 12-Step group and buying a book didn't automatically make my problems vanish. The lure of lust, and my triggers, did not just go away. I often wish that they would, but they don't—even after seven years of working recovery.

Life is filled with nearly constant adversity. Living in an overly sexualized society, it is almost impossible for me to avoid triggering circumstances. Sometimes, just walking through the grocery store past a magazine stand, or seeing someone who is inappropriately dressed may present challenges of lust, objectification, and fantasy. In the past, it was easy to feed my habit of lusting and not recognize what I was doing. But as I began to learn more about what recovery requires, I became more conscious of my thoughts and feelings which included lust, objectification, and fantasy. And then I was ready to learn the power of surrender.

So in this context, *surrender* simply means that I am willing to acknowledge what I am thinking and feeling. It is critical that I am honest with myself about what is taking place in my mind and in my body. Instead of fighting these thoughts by being angry or ashamed of myself, I have learned of a better option, that is to surrender, and then give my feelings over to God. I can choose to be honest with myself, honest with God, and pick up the phone and acknowledge to another person in recovery my powerlessness and my dependence on God's power.

It is interesting to note what happens when I do not want to admit (surrender) these feelings. Typically, I become angry, and distant, and I withdraw emotionally, and these feelings are very disruptive to my serenity. So the key that I have found that encourages me to surrender is to ask myself, *What's really going on inside me?* If I am willing to honestly answer that, and acknowledge feelings of lust, I can be empowered by God to meet the challenges of everyday living. He is pleased with such honesty, and then is able to help me acquire what I really want—a peaceful feeling and genuine recovery.

I now recognize that if I choose not to be honest with myself and say things such as, *I can handle this*, or *It really isn't that big of a deal*, then I nearly always continue to pursue the lustful thought and feeling. So when I choose that option, I choose a path away from recovery. On the other hand, being totally truthful with myself and with others helps me to overcome the power that each incident of lust might otherwise hold over me. I have found that by using this principle daily, I am gaining progressive victory over lust.

I can honestly bear witness that the compulsion to act out subsides dramatically over time. The compulsion to act out is replaced with the feeling that I don't want to act out, because there is something much better—peace and serenity. Cravings to seek out pornography, masturbate, escape by going to adult establishments, or act out with a prostitute no longer hang over me.

In recovery, I now recognize what acting out and feelings of lust really are—a painful escape from reality, with negative consequences that destroy myself and my relationships. But I can choose not to lust. God's power truly does work within me once I surrender and invite Him in. Recovery takes time; it is a slow, deliberate process. Learning to surrender takes practice, but it is worth the effort.

I Am Responsible For My Own Recovery

In addition to turning to God, my spiritual leader, a qualified therapist, and a good 12-Step program (as resources of support and information),

What Can I Do About ~~Him?~~ Me?

the most important key to my success is a willingness to be responsible for my own recovery. When I started on the pathway of recovery seven years ago, I made several boundaries and commitments that would help keep me safe. Let me explain some of them.

One of the boundaries I set is that I will not watch TV by myself. It is amazing how triggering it can be to watch television, alone, flipping through the channels. That is absolutely off limits to me.

Throughout my business life, I felt that it was necessary for me to travel. I traveled all over the world, generally alone. On these trips, I had a lot of free time. Boredom would often trigger lust, and with lust a desire to act out. Now in recovery, I recognize that travel is very dangerous for me, so I choose not to travel alone. I no longer travel unless I am with Rhyll or another traveling companion. In fact, whenever I am traveling without my wife, I request that my business partner and I stay in the same room. Frankly, I don't like to stay in the same room with other guys, but it is a necessary part of my own recovery and safety. I have not traveled alone since 2005. That is a major personal boundary.

Another boundary that is important for my safety is that I choose not to have an Internet connection on my cell phone. It is simply not worth it to me. Sure, it might be fun and maybe even useful to have, but I don't need the temptation of being able to access pornography at any moment.

I also avoid going to triggering places such as water parks and beaches. It is just not worth it to put myself into any situation where I will likely be confronted with circumstances that might provoke me to lust and objectify.

In addition to avoiding the bad by setting boundaries, I also take positive actions to stay in recovery. For example, Rhyll and I pray together each night and morning, and I keep a prayer in my heart during the day.

I also have found it to be rewarding to consistently study the scriptures. One of the great experiences I have is to read the scriptures with the intent of finding what God has to say to me about my recovery, including His love for me, and His power to heal me. I am continually amazed at the personal nature of what the scriptures say to me.

Rhyll and I have committed to check in each night before going to bed. We do what we call the *Vowel Check In*. The vowel "A" stands for *abstinence*. When checking in, abstinence includes disclosing any feelings of lust that I may have experienced during the day. Most days I am able to report that I was free from pursuing feelings of lust. However, it is very important to my recovery and to building trust in our relationship for me to be completely honest in my check-in, and report what have truly been my feelings and actions regarding lust that day.

By seeking out helpful resources, setting boundaries, and taking positive actions, I am able to stay in recovery—one day at a time.

What Can I Do About Our Marriage and Family?

So, what about our marriage? Of course I always knew that what I was doing was wrong and would destroy our marriage. But somehow I was able to compartmentalize my life. I could literally be a different person when I was traveling. When I was home, I would set that person aside, and do my best to be a husband who would provide and protect. We went to church each week; we said prayers as a family each day; we often held family home evening; we occasionally studied the scriptures; and I participated in my church responsibilities. But in all of these activities, I could not really put my heart into them because I knew that I was not being at all honest with myself, with God, and with others.

Perhaps the greatest consequence of my hypocrisy was in my relationship with Rhyll, and my inability to be emotionally available in our marriage. Living a double life is living a lie, a life full of deception. I was just making up stories about what I was doing and how I was feeling, and so I was essentially just going through the motions of being a husband and father. I did not—could not—feel it in my heart.

The more emotion I put into the relationship, as a husband or father, the greater the degree of hypocrisy and pain I would feel. Consequently, in order to protect myself from even more pain and shame, I chose to merely subsist on the surface.

This emotional disconnect was most evident in my relationship with Rhyll. I could communicate with her about the basic mundane things, but I kept myself unavailable emotionally. I could not allow myself to become

What Can I Do About ~~Him?~~ Me?

vulnerable. Vulnerability would also emphasize the hypocrisy and stir up more shame. It is no wonder then, why Rhyll often felt crazy trying to figure out why she was unable to emotionally connect with me; my heart was stone hard, and I was not available. To some extent, I recognized these discordant feelings, but I would work to suppress them.

I had violated trust in all areas of my life. So, in order to save my marriage, it became necessary for me to choose to take charge of my own recovery. I had violated trust hundreds—if not thousands—of times. Working on my own recovery was the only viable option where I could begin to lay a foundation for the possibility of healing our marriage. Any actions of sexual addiction behavior could not exist if I hoped to have a healthy, happy marriage. I had to completely stop acting out, and genuinely seek recovery. I knew that if my addictive behaviors continued, our marriage could never survive. The addiction would win; the marriage would end.

Creating Some Space

After coming forward, I decided that it would be necessary for me to immediately move out of my home. So, on the night of September 11, 2005, I gathered up my things and moved into an old camper in our backyard. I didn't know how long I would be there, but I felt like it might be an opportunity for me to contemplate my circumstances and behavior, and give Rhyll some needed space. I am grateful that she allowed me to stay on the property and interact with the family during the day. While I was on my own in these less than ideal sleeping quarters, I started to count my blessings and recognize all that I was putting at risk by living a life of hypocrisy.

I look back on the weeks and months that I spent in the camper as a very positive experience. I would read my scriptures, say my prayers, and go to sleep. I would get up early and come in the house and shower, and then help prepare breakfast and eat with my family. We would then have family prayer together.

Intimacy needed to be set aside for a time. It was important that we had a separation of both time and space, and that I should not ask for any intimacy. I keenly felt that that was best for both of us, so we were not intimate for several months. That period of abstinence was healthy for both of us. In contrast, years before at the second time that I had come forward, I had felt the need to lean on Rhyll for intimacy immediately, because I was seeking validation from her so that I would feel like I was okay. As I look back on that, it was incredibly unhealthy, unfair, and unwise to expect intimacy with Rhyll at that time.

I am grateful that Rhyll was willing to accept my invitation to continue a weekly date. We generally went out on Friday nights and did something simple, usually dinner and a movie. At first it seemed difficult to get past the wall of fear which all of the lies had brought into our relationship. But gradually over time, and with continued efforts in recovery, our ability to intimately connect improved. As a natural consequence, our sexual relationship and emotional bonding has developed over time as well. I don't recall exactly how long we remained sexually abstinent, or when it was determined that I would come into the bedroom, but it was several months. I am grateful, through recovery, to patiently and respectfully have had the opportunity to re-build intimacy in our relationship.

Choosing to be Open

Along with restoring trust and re-building my relationship with my wife, one of the unexpected blessings that I have found in my recovery has been an openness and deeper connection with my children. They have witnessed the actions of recovery first-hand. I chose to let them be aware of what I was doing, where I was going, what I was reading, which therapists we were meeting with, and what I was learning. They knew when I was going to a 12-Step meeting. They knew when we were going to meet with counselors. My recovery materials were left on the kitchen table and not hidden in a drawer. This openness, and involving our family in our recovery, has created an atmosphere of support in our needs for healing. Transparency with Rhyll and our children has proven to be a great blessing in my own recovery, the recovery in our marriage, and healing in our family.

What Can I Do About ~~Him?~~ *Me?*

There is Hope

Recovery and healing is a spiritual experience. It requires complete honesty with self and others and willingness to acknowledge God's power. Letting God into my life has allowed me to find recovery. Recovery is a process. It takes time. It is worked one day at a time. And it will continue for the rest of my natural life. As I am willing to be honest and turn my will over to God, I believe that all of God's blessings become available to me, to Rhyll, to our marriage, and to our family. I am profoundly grateful for God's boundless grace and healing power. Through all the challenges of working recovery, I have experienced countless blessings and have felt God's love. I am unequivocally committed to continue on the pathway of recovery—one day at a time.

Pathways to Recovery from Sexual Addiction

How does one recover from sexual addiction? One must freely choose for himself or herself to step onto the path of recovery from sexual addiction- and stay on it. The path is narrow and may seem steep at times, so a long-term commitment is vital. Without a firm resolve to "do whatever it takes", discouragement may set in during setbacks, and sadly, a return to illicit sexual behaviors will likely follow.

To step on the path of recovery, the most basic requirements are willingness to surrender to God's will, and courage to be totally honest, accountable and humble.

To stay on the path of recovery, help from others is essential: 1) Seeking spiritual guidance; 2) Working with a qualified therapist; 3) Working the 12 Steps and 4) Educating themselves.

The Solution for Sexual Addiction

The solution begins with the heart. Faith, honesty, admission that life has become unmanageable, recognition that assistance from others is required, and a willingness to take sustained action are all requirements in the work of recovery.

Making the Decision

Because the problems with sexual addiction are fourfold (physical, spiritual, emotional and social), healing must also come about in these four areas.

The crucial change in attitude began when we admitted we were powerless, that our habit had us whipped. [With faith, we took the actions of recovery,] we came to meetings and withdrew from our habit…; this meant no sex with self or others…[and not viewing pornography].

We discovered that we could stop, that not feeding the hunger didn't kill us, that sex was indeed optional. There was hope for freedom, and we began

---

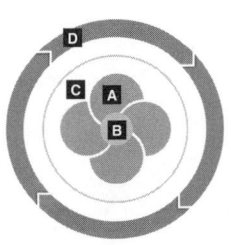

* Explanation of the Circular Models:

A The 4 petals within each model represents an individual – as a physical, emotional, spiritual & mental being or entity.

B The center of the circle indicates the primary focus of the heart.

C The white area enveloping the 4 petals represents a person's thoughts, behaviors & emotions.

D And the outermost circle represents actions, outreach & responses.

to feel alive. Encouraged to continue, we turned more and more away from our isolating obsession with sex and self and turned to God and others.

All this was scary. We couldn't see the pathway ahead, except that others had gone that way before. Each new step of surrender felt it would be off the edge into oblivion, but we took it. And instead of killing us, surrender was killing the obsession! We had stepped into the light, into a whole new way of life...and the healing began. (White Book p. 204)

What I Can Do

WHAT ABOUT THE KIDS?

Telling our children, and their reactions over the last seven years

By Rhyll Croshaw

I am the mother of seven amazing children, and grandmother to 14 beautiful grandchildren. My commitment to motherhood and family is foremost in my life, and it always has been. Early on in my husband's addiction, we had precious little information or help with our individual afflictions, our marriage, or in raising our children to be balanced and—healthy despite the underlying influence of pornography and sexual addiction in our home. Although I highly valued my children's development and safety, I did not know how my husband's addiction might influence them; and I did not know if—or how—it should best be addressed with the children. Here I would like to share how my children fared based on the information we followed at the time, how sexual addiction of a parent negatively influences children, and how parents might handle this situation better than we did.

I am frequently asked about how our children responded during this crisis, and how they are doing now. As I explained in my story, our children knew very little about their dad's behaviors and how it was affecting our marriage until his third disclosure to me. At that point, our children were more mature—five were married and the twins were 15. Steven determined that our children should know, and I agreed. We have since realized that this became an important part of our healing. I was grateful that he was willing to talk openly with them. Such honesty had to be there for all of us, and it needed to continue. This honesty laid a foundation of trust between Steven and the rest of the family. As a family, we continue to talk about recovery, and strive to foster these feelings of openness in our relationships.

Professionals in the sex addiction treatment field believe that children should be told about addictions that are occurring in the family. More on that is included below. "A family is only as sick as its darkest secrets."[47] We found that Steven's disclosure to our children helped mend rifts between him and the children, and it helped the children to grow and develop in positive ways as well.

Of course, there are many adverse effects of pornography and sexual addiction on children. Most children can sense that something is wrong in the home when mom and dad are fighting or ignoring each other. Every child needs to feel safe in the family unit in order to thrive and grow physically, emotionally, and spiritually. Children may also perceive a disconnect between themselves and the addicted person due to the addict's mismanagement of emotions. The combination of uncertainty between the parents and emotional distance from the addicted parent, can create feelings of anxiety in children, as well as a lack of belonging and safety. When there is anxiety and uncertainty in a child's life, it is harmful to her progression because she will either internalize the negative feelings by blaming herself, or act out these feelings by behaving inappropriately.

One seemingly obvious concern for children is that living with an addict in the home often exposes the child to attitudes of disrespect and even abuse towards women. There is also a very real risk that the child may be exposed to pornography—even accidentally—that has been viewed at home. Such exposure, and then the tendency of hiding the exposure, may escalate the child's behavior into a full-blown addiction before any adults, including parents, are even aware. Most adult addicts report viewing pornography for the first time around nine or ten years old, and many in their own home. Because sexual addiction tends to run in families, we often see multiple generations in families that suffer from the destruction caused by this addiction.

Suggestions for parents who are concerned about telling their children come from professionals and from my own experience. First, it is highly

---

47 Catherine McCall June 1, 2011, *Psychology Today*.

recommended that the children know what is going on. "Disclosure should come from the addict in an appropriate way, without specifics and without making a visual image. And, if possible, the spouse should be present. Keep in mind that such a disclosure should be made at developmentally appropriate ages. In time, as parents exhibit signs of recovery and encourage ongoing openness and a loving attitude that they are available to the child, there will likely be ongoing healing in the family."[48] Most sex addict treatment professionals suggest mid-adolescence as an appropriate age for disclosure.

It is also important to teach children about joys of healthy sexuality in a developmentally appropriate and non-shaming way. The sexuality education they get from home should also include information about the dangers and consequences of pornography and sexual addiction.

Most fathers or mothers have a very difficult time wanting to share any information about their sexual addiction issues with their children. This attitude is understandable since there is so much shame connected with this behavior. And who wants to look bad in front of their children! Nevertheless, parents, and especially the offending parent who has betrayed marriage vows, need to be aware that their attitudes and even many of their behaviors have already been viewed and felt by their children—even prior to any formal disclosure. The lasting damage may have already been done. Honest, humble, age-appropriate disclosure that also shows a change of heart and lifestyle, can restore children to a sense of equilibrium and safety after a grieving time.

Finally, may I add that the most surprising outcome of my husband's honest and humble disclosure to our children was the strengthening and unifying effect that it has had on our children as they have watched my husband and me faithfully work on our own recoveries.

Each mother and father should be prayerful in the timing, motivation, and appropriateness of sharing these sensitive matters; but for my husband, my children, and me, these experiences seem to have strengthened and unified us as a family, for which we are grateful. The following story we

---

48 Black C., Dillon D., Carnes S., 2003, *Sexual Addiction and Compulsivity*, 10:67

would like to share is from our daughter Tara, who is married and has her own young family now.

What I Can Do

TARA'S STORY

I am the daughter of a recovering sex addict. My story isn't all that dramatic. I might even venture that in a peculiar way this challenge has been among the greatest blessings of my life. Given the option, I don't think I would have chosen of myself to pass over this mountain; however, the lessons I have learned as a result of this experience are proving to bless myself and family in unexpected ways.

Growing up, I didn't feel any different from other children. In fact, I counted myself uniquely blessed. I was loved, well provided for, and had an abundance of opportunity to develop my interests and talents. I seemed to have a wellspring of confidence at my core. As a result, I fared well in my pursuits academically and socially.

I recall feeling close to my mom through my formative years. She was my primary confidant and mentor. In contrast, I occasionally talked with my dad but on a superficial level, and rarely sought him out for emotional support. This was mostly due to the fact that he was often working long hours or away on business. When he was home he felt distant to me—rarely speaking of himself or engaging me in conversation about my activities and interests. In spite of this, I did believe he loved me and I thought that my relationship with my dad was normal.

I have only vague recollections as a young child of challenges in my parents' marriage. Any issues they had were discussed behind closed doors. It wasn't until high school when I really began to see something amiss in my parents' relationship. I recall occasionally worrying about the prospect of my parents separating, but the feeling didn't linger. Full of grit, my mom was generally upbeat and positive. In my opinion she did a tremendous job of maintaining the household and keeping everything and everyone in order.

What Can I Do About ~~Him?~~ Me?

Yet as I grew older and became more perceptive, I noticed that something weighed heavily on her. Finances were a constant concern during this period, but I felt there was something deeper causing her anxiety.

As I entered my older teen years and began interacting more with my friends' fathers, I noticed the level of warmth and emotional closeness some of them shared with their dads. It was then that I started to recognize how much was missing in my own father-daughter relationship. I didn't realize it at the time, but for many years I didn't know my father. In his shame-based Jekyll and Hyde life, he was limited in his capacity to love and be loved.

In my concern, I began soliciting my mom for information so I could provide some emotional support. She would never go into detail about my father's behavior, but it soon became clear to me that Dad had a problem—the extent of which I didn't learn until later. The hardest thing for me at the time was seeing my mom suffer. She was clearly in pain, but there was little I could do for her.

I soon graduated from high school and moved away from home. Preoccupied with college and other activities I was home only occasionally, and for a time was oblivious to the trouble brewing between my parents.

It all came to a head years later, only months after I was married. It was a pleasant Sunday afternoon. Just after we arrived at my parents' home, my dad ushered my husband and me outside, sat us down, and proceeded to tell us of his shocking behaviors that had led up to his recent arrest. I was devastated. I felt anger, sadness, and a deep sense of betrayal.

Despite my anger and sadness, I was able that night to put my arms around my dad, tell him I loved him, and forgive him. I credit myself very little for this frank forgiveness. First of all, my father had demonstrated forgiveness and patience for me on previous occasions, softening my heart toward him. I also believe my ability to forgive him was a gift from God.

Second, the way my mom was choosing to deal with the situation diffused much of my own anger. She wasn't bitter and dramatic. She calmly sat next to him and through glossy eyes said that she was going to try and support my dad as he worked toward recovery of his addiction. I decided that if she could forgive him—one who had suffered so directly and deeply as a result of his choices—I could do as much. She did, however, make it clear that she wouldn't support him in his addiction if he continued to act out. I recall her saying that "she would see how things went" as my dad behaved in a way that could start rebuilding her trust.

I won't pretend that all my anger and sadness were gone that day. As the days and weeks passed, there were times when those feelings would resurface and I would vent to my husband or call on a Higher Power for help as I waded through my grief and fear. Even though my dad was doing well in his recovery, I knew there weren't any guarantees for him or my parents' marriage. But on the whole, I marvel at how easily I was able to forgive him and move forward. Doing so freed me from the debilitating effects of resentment, shame, and bitterness that have overcome some individuals in similar situations.

Over six years later, I look back and am grateful for the lessons I have learned through this experience. I have learned not to be so afraid of this issue. I may, as a mother, deal with this in some form with my own children. Yet I feel like I can face this potential problem with courage because I now have the education and tools to help me. I know that recovery from pornography and sex addiction is possible. I have witnessed it! I used to be so black and white in my thinking, certain that if I or others messed up, that was it—there was no going back. But that isn't true. Change is possible for each of us, no matter what our unique challenge or weakness might be.

My father has worked tirelessly over the past several years to stay on the road of recovery. He is doing remarkably well, and in the process is helping many others with this same issue. Recovery is a daily effort for anyone battling through this difficulty. It is at times a challenge for both my parents as they continue to work toward recovery as individuals and as a couple. But through their faith and steady effort, they are growing together each day and are happier in their marriage than I have ever seen them.

What I Can Do

RECOVERY ROAD MAPS

Road Map 1: Is He Working Recovery?

Road Map 2: Am I Working Recovery?

Road Map 3: Recovery For an Individual

Road Map 4: Healing for the Afflicted Spouse

Road Map 5: Saving the Marriage

Road Map 1: *Is He Working Recovery?*

I am not serious about changing if:	I am serious about changing if:
I lie, am evasive, or disclose information only when asked.	I am honest and open.
I was caught or reported by someone else, rather than admitting to or confessing inappropriate behavior.	I am open and willing to talk about what I do, think, and feel.
I pretend or try to convince others that there are no problems, that they are taken care of, or are no big deal.	I am trying to find out what led me to my addictions and prevent addictive behavior from happening again.
I am defensive, deny, minimize, rationalize, or blame others in order to avoid dealing with my problems.	I take full responsibility for making personal changes.
I want to go back to the way things were before getting caught, rather than improving and growing.	I have made up my own rules for staying out of compulsive sexual behaviors and am following them.
I refuse to attend 12-Step meetings or get a sponsor, and continue to "punish" myself.	I regularly attend 12-Step groups, report to my sponsor, and accept God's forgiveness in my life.
I am not willing to put in the time or effort to fix problems or work the 12-Steps.	I am working on the 12-Steps and my issues daily.
I run away, hide, or won't talk about my behaviors, feelings, thoughts, and fantasies.	I meet regularly with my ecclesiastical leader.
I do not actively participate in counseling.	I decide to see a counselor on my own rather than being forced to or told to by someone else.
I use other addictions—such as alcohol or drugs—to avoid dealing with my real problems.	I go to professional counseling sessions, work on issues underlying my behavior, and do all homework given.

(Road Map 1, continued)

I am not serious about changing if:	I am serious about changing if:
I act as if I am the victim and seek sympathy, or try to get others to take sides.	I am working more on what I need to change rather than on what I think my spouse needs to change.
I want my spouse to be okay with my addictions and I feel cheated if I can't continue in them.	I give my spouse the space and closeness she needs.
I criticize and blame others more than I take personal responsibility.	I show that I understand the hurt which I have caused my spouse and loved ones.
I am angry, moody, resentful, critical, or out of control, and only think about my own needs.	I work to earn others' trust and forgiveness.
I try to make a quick-fix deal and apologize—just to have the issue dropped.	I work to solve problems that were caused by my addiction.
I am manipulative and use fear, guilt, or threats to get what I want.	I speak and act with respect.
I make impulsive decisions and have impulsive behaviors.	I am dependable in taking care of my family, occupation, and religious responsibilities.
I make promises rather than changes.	I am setting specific, measurable goals and achieving them.
I am not living standards in accordance with my religious beliefs.	I am living the standards of my religious beliefs.
I continue to put myself in situations where I'll be tempted.	I have made significant lifestyle changes.

Road Map 2: *Am I Working Recovery?*

I am probably not making needed changes if:	I am making effective changes if:
I feel that in some way my spouse's addiction is my fault and blame myself for his behavior.	I recognize that pornography addiction is a serious problem and requires hard work to find recovery. However, I do not blame myself for my spouse's addiction.
I pretend there isn't a problem, it is already taken care of, or it isn't a big deal.	I require honesty and transparency from my spouse and ask him directly when something is bothering me.
I believe whatever my spouse tells me, even if my gut tells me something is wrong.	I take responsibility for making positive changes in my life based on the feelings of my heart and the instincts of my gut.
I refuse to take responsibility for changing what I can and taking care of myself.	I find help and support from others in dealing with the betrayal and trauma I am experiencing and its impact on me.
I try to deal with my emotions on my own.	I openly share what I think, feel, and am experiencing with appropriate trusted people.
I keep the addiction a secret and fail to seek outside help.	I meet regularly with my ecclesiastical leader.
I think that only my spouse needs counseling—not me; or, I fail to do homework and skip sessions.	I work with a therapist who is trained in sexual addiction—whether or not my spouse wants me to.
I make excuses for not attending 12-Step meetings for spouses, or quit going once I feel okay again.	I actively attend 12-Step meetings for spouses and work on my own recovery daily.
I rationalize that I don't really need any guidance.	I find a sponsor and work with her regularly.
I neglect or minimize my needs and wants.	I practice self-care daily.
I bury my emotions, or utilize other addictions such as food or drugs to avoid them.	I allow myself to feel natural emotions, hurt, and anger, and then surrender them to God.

(Road Map 2, continued)

I am probably not making needed changes if:	I am making effective changes if:
I persist in believing that God doesn't care about me.	I seek to feel God's love for me.
I deny, minimize, rationalize, or blame others to avoid making changes or letting go of resentment.	I work towards forgiving and letting go of the resentment for the hurt which my spouse has caused.
I criticize or blame my spouse—rather than set boundaries or make changes to protect myself.	I set and follow boundaries to protect myself from my spouse's addictive behavior and from obsessing about his addiction.
I make a quick-fix deal: If my spouse says he is sorry, I will just forget it and won't talk about it anymore.	I refuse to accept or enable addict behavior; I look for positive changes—not just promises.
I obsess about what my spouse needs to do, rather than work on my own recovery.	I focus on the changes that I can make, rather than on what I think my spouse needs to change.
I choose how to act based on fear of my spouses reaction, or I respond explosively.	I appropriately share my needs and feelings with the addict instead of worrying about how he might respond.
I set my level of affection based on what my spouse wants rather than on what I need.	I ask for the space, closeness, or help that I need.
I go along with addictive behavior, or tell myself that it is okay—or that it is not really that bad.	I work towards extending trust if my spouse is showing behavior that is deserving of trust.
I use demands, fear, guilt, manipulation, or threats to get what I want or need.	I take care of my personal and family needs.
I do it all myself—even if I'm overwhelmed, and constantly demand perfection from myself.	I set small measurable goals for myself and work for progress—not perfection.
I do not put in the time and effort to deal with the problem, or fail to set realistic expectations.	I accept that healing from the effects of my spouse's addiction is a long process that will take time and effort.

Road Map 3: Recovery for an Individual

Goal: Restore self-respect and wholeness

1. **Decide to Fully Commit to Actions of Recovery**
   - Recognize the reality of the pornography/sexual addiction.
   - Progress will occur when a decision is made to fully commit to actions of recovery.
   - Seek God's help; He will help you.

2. **Come Out of Hiding**
   - Complete, honest disclosure to spouse, clergy leader, and qualified therapist is necessary.

3. **Set Safe Boundaries and Self Care**
   - Set safe boundaries (for example, no private use of computer or television).
   - Daily physical and spiritual care: exercise, healthy diet, adequate rest, positive affirmations.

4. **Gain Knowledge**
   - Learn about sexual addiction.
   - Learn what recovery requires and the attributes of genuine recovery.
   - Short-term sobriety (abstinence) does not indicate recovery.
   - Full recovery is a life-time process.
   - Learn how to support your spouse's healing.

5. **Clergy Involvement**
   - Frequent accountability visits with an informed ecclesiastical leader.

6. **Qualified Counseling**
   - Genuine commitment to on-going counseling from a qualified therapist (typical minimum is 18 months).

7. **Join 12-Step Fellowship for Sexual Addiction Recovery**
   - Join a 12-Step Fellowship for sexual addiction, find a sponsor, and work all 12 Steps. Commit to long-term—perhaps lifetime—involvement.

8. **Recovery is a Spiritual Process**
   - Willingly acknowledge that alone, a person is powerless over their addiction.
   - Come to believe that a Power greater than oneself can restore wholeness to life.
   - We must turn our will and life over to that Power.

Road Map 4: Healing for the Afflicted Spouse

Goal: Restore serenity and wholeness

1. **Recognize Your Own Need for Healing**
   - Recognize your trauma as the afflicted spouse of an individual addicted to pornography.
   - Seek God's help; He will help you.

2. **Talk with Others**
   - Interact with an ecclesiastical leader.
   - Communicate with a qualified therapist.
   - Develop a support system.

3. **Join a 12-Step Fellowship**
   - Find a sponsor
   - Work all 12 Steps diligently.

4. **Self Care**
   - Slow down. Allow time for healing before making life-changing decisions (1 year minimum). If you are at risk, decisions may need to be made more quickly.
   - Prayerfully set boundaries defining unacceptable behavior in order to protect your emotional, physical, and spiritual well-being.
   - Daily physical and spiritual care: exercise, healthy diet, adequate rest, spiritually-centering activities.

5. **Education**
   - Fully recognize that you are not the cause of your spouse's addiction, and that you cannot "fix" or control your spouse.
   - Learn more about the nature of pornography/sexual addiction and how it impacts you.

- Learn what is required to experience healing as the spouse of one addicted.

6. **Support Spouse's Recovery**
   - Make very clear to your spouse that you will support his/her genuine commitment to recovery, but will not enable continued addictive behaviors.

7. **Healing is a Spiritual Process**
   - Willingly acknowledge that you are powerless over your spouse's actions; you can influence, but you cannot control.
   - Believe that a Power greater than you can restore you to wholeness; turn your life over to that Power.

Road Map 5: Saving the Marriage

Goal: Restore connection and wholeness

1. **Recognize That the Marriage Relationship Is Affected**
   - Trust has been violated. The marriage may be intact, but it is not whole. Even if the marriage relationship is recoverable, it will not happen immediately.
   - Genuine recovery of a marriage relationship takes time. There is no universal rule regarding how long it may take. Follow your instincts.
   - If you desire to save your marriage, seek out a qualified counselor trained in sexual addiction.

2. **Working on Recovery Allows Marriage to Heal**
   - A healthy, whole marriage cannot coexist with sexually addictive behavior. If the addiction continues, the marriage will never be whole; the addiction will always win.

3. **Work on Individual Recovery and Healing**
   - Recovery of the marriage relationship follows continued individual recoveries, and healing from the trauma of addiction.

4. **Reach Out to Each Other**
   - Notice ways in which your spouse is trying to reach out for connection. Respond to such efforts with honesty.

5. **Build True Intimacy**
   - In recovery, a one-dimensional physical relationship is replaced with an intimate social, emotional, spiritual, and sexual bonding.
   - Spend time together to develop a holistic relationship (walking, gardening, cooking, etc.).

6. **Nurture Others**
   - Children need extra love and attention. They may also be suffering and are in need of healing.
   - Needed personal renewal will be found in small acts of service.

What I Can Do

RESOURCES I CAN RECOMMEND

Web Sites

www.rhyllrecovery.org
www.salifeline.org
www.sanon.org

Books

After the Affair by Janis Abrahms Spring

Boundaries: When to Say Yes, When to Say No—to Take Control of Your Life by Henry Cloud & John Townsend

Codependent No More: How To Stop Controlling Others and Start Caring for Yourself by Melody Beattie

From Heartache to Healing: Finding Power In Christ to Deal With A Loved One's Sexual Addiction (2010), Colleen C. & Philip A. Harrison

He Restoreth My Soul: Understanding Pornography and Breaking the Chemical and Spiritual Chains of Pornography Addiction Through the Atonement of Jesus Christ (2010), Donald L. Hilton, Jr. M.D.

Healing the Shame that Binds You by John Bradshaw

How Can I Forgive You? The Courage to Forgive, the Freedom Not To by Janis Abrahms Spring

Lord I Believe; Help Thou Mine Unbelief: A Workbook Approach (2005), Rod W. Jeppsen

Love You, Hate the Porn: Healing a Relationship Damaged by Virtual Infidelity by Mark Chamberlain & Geoff Steurer

Mending a Shattered Heart by Stefanie Carnes

S-Anon 12-Steps, S-Anon Literature [for the loved ones of sexual addicts] www.sanon.org

The Gifts Of Imperfection: Let Go of Who You Think You're Supposed To Be and Embrace Who You Are by Brene Brown

Understanding Pornography and Sexual Addiction, produced by S.A. Lifeline Foundation

Your Sexually Addicted Spouse: How Partners Can Cope and Heal (2009), Barbara Steffens & Marsha Means

Audio CDs

Strengthening Recovery Through Strengthening Marriage; 6-part audio program by Geoff Steurer and Kevin Skinner

DVDs

The Heart of the Matter; honest, powerful portrait of what it means to be a Christian addicted to pornography. A film by Jessica Mockett, directed by Jessica Mockett and edited by Nathan D. Lee. www.theheartofthemattermovie.com

Pornography and the Brain by Donald L. Hilton, Jr. M.D.

Healing Relationships Damaged by Pornography by Geoff Steurer

Pornography, the Great Lie: A Guide for Families of All Faiths, published by Deseret Book

Locating a Therapist

"Find a therapist" link on *www.salifeline.org*

About the Author

Rhyll Anne Croshaw is a highly sought after speaker, having spoken at BYU Women's Conference and many community and church events on the subject of pornography, sexual addiction and betrayal trauma recovery. She and her husband Steven are the founders of SA Lifeline Foundation, a non-profit foundation dedicated to providing individuals, couples and families hope for recovery from sexual addiction and betrayal trauma through education, supporting 12-Step recovery groups, encouraging spiritual guidance, and emphasizing qualified therapy. For more information go to www.salifeline.org.

Rhyll graduated from Brigham Young University at the relatively young age of 58, where she earned a BS degree in Family Life.

A piano and music teacher from the time she was 16, she still loves to use her talents and education in piano and choral instruction as often as possible.

Rhyll has been married to Steven Croshaw for 43 years and is the proud mother of 7 children and 21 grandchildren.

At rhyllrecovery.com you will find videos made by Rhyll, Blog posts and answers to pertinent questions about women's healing and recovery.